The Brown Paper School presents

My Backyard History Book

written by
DAVID WEITZMAN

illustrated by
JAMES ROBERTSON

Little, Brown and Company
Boston Toronto

The Brown Paper School is a series of small books about big ideas, written and designed for kids and grownups together. The series comes from a group of California teachers, writers and artists who get together every now and then to work on stuff for kids and to have a good time. They believe learning only happens when it is wanted; that it can happen anywhere and doesn't require fancy tools. This book and the others in the series are dedicated to anyone who thinks so too.

Other books in The Brown Paper School series:

The I Hate Mathematics! Book by Marilyn Burns
The Reasons for Seasons, by Linda Allison

The Brown Paper School series was edited and prepared for publication at The Yolla Bolly Press in Covelo, California, between September 1974 and January 1975. The series is under the editorial direction of James Robertson. The staff for the series is: Carolyn Robertson, Cindy Boatwright, Colleen Carter, Sharon Miley, Sadako McInerney.

Acknowledgments appear on page 128.

Published simultaneously in Canada by
Little, Brown & Company (Canada) Limited.
Printed in the United States of America. T 08/75
D   B B
Library of Congress Cataloging in Publication Data

Weitzman, David L
  My backyard history book.

  (The brown paper school)
  SUMMARY: Activities and projects, such as making time capsules and rubbings and tracing genealogy, demonstrate that learning about the past begins at home.
    1. United States—History, Local—Juvenile lit-
erature. 2. Local history—Juvenile literature.
[1. History. 2. Local history. 3. United States
—History, Local] I. Robertson, James
II. Title
E178.3.W45 1975   973'.07   75-6577
ISBN 0-316-92901-8

What's in this book

This book is about you

and your grandfather

and his grandmother

and the songs they used to sing

and picnics

and the wagon they used to drive

and the house where your mother was born

and the uncle on your mother's side that everyone used to whisper about.

This book is about attics
and your father's grandfather's famous horse.

It's about long ago

and not so long ago —

big things

little things

and all the things

that make the history of your place

and your people

and you

special.

Whatshisname

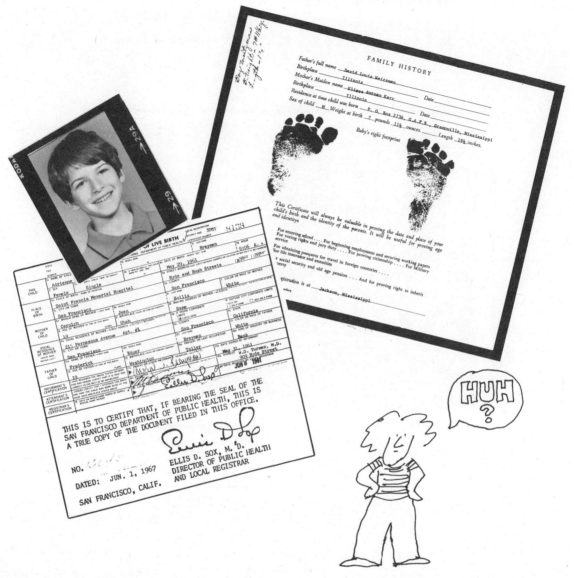

Have you ever looked at your name? *Really* looked at it? Sure, you put it on papers at school — and it always turns up on your grade report. (Even when you wish it wouldn't, right?) But have you ever tried to figure out what it means, or where it came from in the first place? Do you know who gave you your name, or whose name it might have been before it was given to you? Names seem like such everyday common things that we don't think about them very much; but every name has a history, and here's how to find out all about yours.

On the next few pages you can find out a little about the story of names, how they all came about, and why we have them; and from this you can reconstruct the history of your own name and even help your friends figure out theirs. (You might even start a business like Namefinders, Inc. or Whatshisname.)

Be sure to put down all your names. Most people have three names, but you may have more that you don't know about (and which will probably show up on your birth certificate). Your last name, or surname, is probably the same as your father's and his father's. You should also find out your mother's surname before she was married (maiden name) so that you can find out about the origins of her name too. (Hint: she may be using it as her middle name now.) If you are Spanish, or if your mother and father decided to put their names together with a hyphen, your name might contain both your parents' surnames.

Names are very special kinds of words, carrying with them a lot of information about your past, like your ancestors' nationality, their first occupation, perhaps even their appearance, reputation, or the place where they first lived.

One of the reasons we don't give much thought to our names is because everyone has one. But that wasn't always true. If you go back far enough into history, three or four hundred years, you'd find that while everyone had first names like Maria, or Robert, or Wilhelm, or Yvonne, or Ravi, few people had surnames. They didn't need them. Villages were so small that everybody knew everyone else, and last names just weren't necessary. In fact, many of the people in the village were probably part of one large family anyway.

But then things changed. Settlements got bigger. Some people lived in big cities and it became more difficult to keep track of everyone (particularly for the tax collector). So if you were new in town and you asked who that was going down the street, the answer might be, "Oh, that's John, William's son," or "James the baker," or "Keith from the hill." So it became customary to have a first name with a description tacked onto it to distinguish which of the many Williams, or Roberts, or Anns, or Catherines you were.

IT'S A LITTLE LIKE BEING IN MRS. HESTON'S FIFTH GRADE CLASS AND THERE ARE 3 SUSANS BESIDES YOU! (MAKES YOU FEEL KIND OF ORDINARY)

SUSAN, CAN YOU TELL THE CLASS ABOUT YOUR SUMMER?

HOW DO YOU THINK EVERYONE WOULD TELL ONE FROM THE OTHER? USE LAST NAMES? HOW ABOUT USING NICK-NAMES?

SUZY THE FOX — GOODIE SUE — BIG SUE

(AND SO FORTH)

HOW ABOUT YOU? DO YOU HAVE A NICKNAME? IF YOU DON'T AND WANT ONE — GO AHEAD. WHAT WILL IT BE?

The idea of everyone in the same family having the same surname was a later development, and for a while families living under one roof might all have different last names. Here's an example of an imaginary family from the Middle Ages showing how the idea of surnames got started.

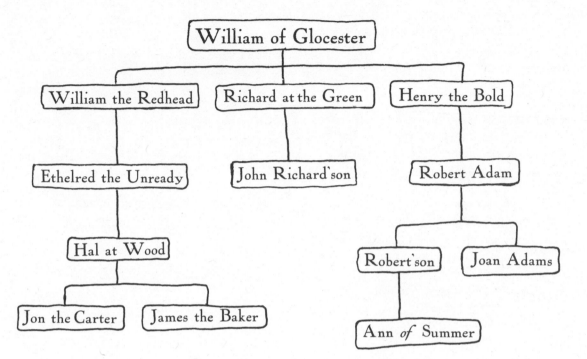

That's how the custom of giving surnames began. People were identified with their father by his name, a *patronym*; or by a descriptive nickname; or by where they lived; or even by the time of year of their births; and often by what they did, their occupations. Your name probably fits into one of these categories, so let's see which one.

Robert*son*	Davi*son*
Carl*son*	*ibn* Hussein
Robin*son*	*Ben*-David
Steven*s*	Rodrig*uez*
Richard*son*	*O*'Reilly
*Mac*Andrew	Pavlo*vitch*

In the late Middle Ages, one of the easiest ways to identify yourself was with your father. So, when asked, you said you were:

One of your ancestors might have had some physical feature or reputation to which his friends (or enemies) referred when they spoke of him, like:

Youngman	Black
Strong	Altman (*old man*)
Newman	Moody
Klein (*small*)	Good
Armstrong	Truman
Goodfriend	Hardy

Or maybe you became known by the time of year or even the events which occurred on the date of your birth, or the names of saints whose day you might have been born on:

Summer	Noel
Winter	Valentine

(Saint) Martin, Martini, or Martinez

Where you lived was also a convenient way to refer to who you were, like:

Green	Woods
Wells	Atwater
Underwood	

Occupation, even today, is the way most people describe themselves. A man might have been referred to as "John the . . . "

Miller	Baker
Smith	Mason
Schumacher	Farmer
Carter	Barber
Piper	Plowman
Brewer	Archer

A TEST!

YES, FOLKS, HERE IT IS. RIGHT AT THE START, YOUR VERY OWN PERSONAL HISTORY TEST SEE HOW MUCH YOU KNOW ABOUT YOUR OWN PAST —

CHEER UP. YOU GET TO GRADE IT YOURSELF.

BUT DON'T ASK YOUR PARENTS ANY OF THE QUESTIONS UNTIL YOU HAVE TRIED IT BY YOURSELF. READY? START!

1 WHAT IS YOUR FATHER'S FULL NAME? (FIRST, LAST AND ANYTHING BETWEEN)

C'MON KID!

2 WHERE WAS HE BORN? TOWN, STATE OR COUNTRY.

GOO!

3 WHAT IS HIS BIRTHDATE? DAY, MONTH AND THE YEAR.

4 WHAT IS YOUR MOTHER'S FULL NAME? FIRST, LAST, MIDDLE & MAIDEN NAME. (HER LAST NAME BEFORE SHE WAS MARRIED.)

5 WHERE WAS SHE BORN? TOWN, COUNTRY OR STATE. REMEMBER, NO FAIR ASKING ANYONE ELSE!

6 WHAT IS HER BIRTHDATE? DOES SHE TRY TO KEEP IT A SECRET?

7 WHAT ARE THE NAMES OF YOUR GRANDFOLKS?

(FATHER'S FATHER, FATHER'S MOTHER, MOTHER'S FATHER, MOTHER'S MOTHER.)

HUH?

8 WHERE (TOWN, STATE OR COUNTRY) AND WHEN (YEAR AT LEAST) WERE EACH OF YOUR GRANDPARENTS BORN?

9 WHAT ARE (OR WERE) THE OCCUPATIONS OF ALL YOUR GRANDPARENTS.

10 FROM WHICH COUNTRY DID YOUR FATHER'S FAMILY COME ORIGINALLY? (UNLESS YOU ARE A NATIVE AMERICAN, THEY CAME FROM SOMEWHERE ELSE.)

DON'T GIVE UP YET! THERE IS MORE ON THE NEXT PAGE →

11 FROM WHICH COUNTRY DID YOUR MOTHER'S FAMILY COME ORIGINALLY? (IS THERE A CLUE IN ONE OF THOSE FAMILY NAMES?)

12 WHEN DID YOUR ANCESTORS (ON BOTH SIDES) FIRST COME TO THIS COUNTRY?

OH, ABOUT 12 O'CLOCK.

13 WHERE DID THEY LAND WHEN THEY ARRIVED IN THIS COUNTRY?

14 WHERE WAS THE FIRST PLACE THEY SETTLED? (TOWN OR STATE).

15 WHICH CITIES AND STATES HAS YOUR FAMILY LIVED IN? (BOTH SIDES)

OH NO!

16 HOW DID THE TOWN YOU LIVE IN (NEAR) HAPPEN TO GET ITS NAME?

17 WHO AND WHAT LIVED THERE BEFORE IT BECAME A TOWN OR A CITY?

18 WHY DOES YOUR TOWN HAPPEN TO BE WHERE IT IS?

THE END

NOW CHECK YOUR ANSWERS WITH SOMEONE ELSE. (YOU MAY HAVE TROUBLE FINDING ANYONE WHO KNOWS THEM ALL.) GIVE YOURSELF ONE POINT FOR EACH ANSWER THAT IS CORRECT OR MOSTLY CORRECT OR PARTLY CORRECT.

15 OR MORE POINTS } CONGRATULATIONS, YOU'RE ALREADY A BACKYARD HISTORIAN.

10 OR MORE — GOOD BUT YOU CAN DO BETTER

5 OR MORE (OR LESS!) OOPS!

DON'T FEEL BADLY IF YOUR SCORE IS LOW! NO ONE KNOWS VERY MUCH ABOUT THEIR OWN HISTORY. IF THEY DID, WE WOULD HAVE HAD NO REASON TO WRITE THIS BOOK!

TO PROVE IT, GIVE THE SAME TEST TO SOME GROWN-UP FRIEND (BET THEY DO CRUMMY!)

Getting a line on your past

Before too many years of your life accumulate, maybe it would be a good idea to sit down a minute and remember those that have already gone by. An easy way to reconstruct your life is to make a time line showing the events most important to you. Think it's easy? Let's see how much you remember about you.

Get a long piece of paper, or tape two or three pieces of writing paper together in a line. Draw a horizontal line across the paper in about the middle.

Divide the line with a mark for each year of your life, beginning with your first birthday at the left, and move across until you come to today.

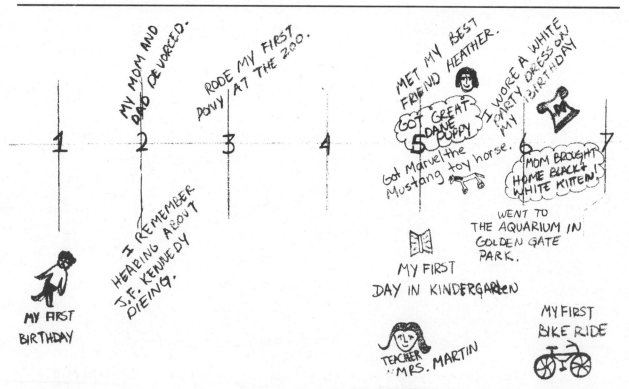

Here is a time line that was done by a friend. After you have done yours, ask your parents

18

Write in, above and below the line, all the events of your life that you can remember. Since there have been so many, you might start with these . . .

your birthday

the very first thing you remember happening

your first toys

when you began school (What was your kindergarten teacher's name?)

the first book you read by yourself

the year you learned to ride a bike, ice skate, play a musical instrument, swim, or whistle

a train, airplane, or car ride somewhere

the time you broke your arm falling off your bicycle

the year your voice changed or you grew really fast

when you met your best friend

the first movie, baseball game, concert, or play you ever went to

when your bedtime changed so that you could stay up late

when your first tooth fell out

elementary school graduation

You may want to put your time line on the wall. Add paper to it from time to time to keep it up to date, and fill in other things as you remember them.

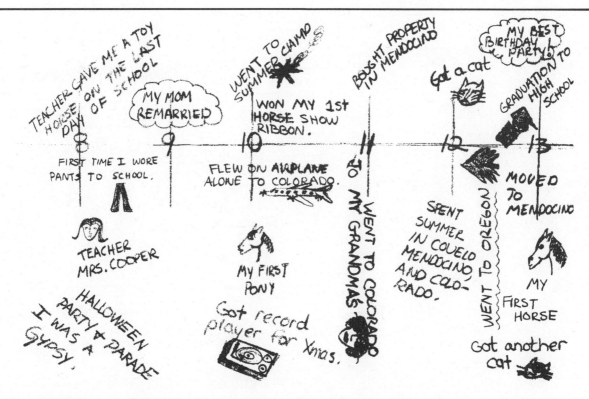

what is the very first thing they remember. See whose memory is strongest in the family.

HERE IS SOMETHING SPECIAL TO DO ON YOUR BIRTHDAY BESIDES EAT TOO MUCH ICECREAM AND DUTCH FUDGE BIRTHDAY CAKE WITH PEPPERMINT CRUNCH ICING AND LITTLE CANDIES ALL OVER THE TOP. SOMETHING TO DO THAT IS

A LITTLE BIT SECRET— YOU DO IT BY YOUR- SELF AND PUT IT AWAY FOR A LONG, LONG TIME AND DON'T TELL ANY- ONE WHAT IS INSIDE IT. WHAT IS INSIDE WHAT? THE THING YOU HAVE MADE —

A birthday time capsule

Here's something to do on your next birthday. Make a time capsule and put lots of things in it, some important, some unimportant, which together will make a record of the year. A time capsule could be a shoe box or paper carton; but if your home is small, it will get really cozy after about a dozen years of you and your brothers and sisters storing time capsules all over the place, so your capsule may just be an envelope. Don't think about it too hard, because you never know what you'll enjoy pulling out of the capsule a year or five years from now. Just take a couple hours on your birthday to go through your stuff and pick out a few things to be put into the capsule.

Some items that might be included:

snapshots of family, friends, and pets made during the year

school pictures of you, or one of those little photo strips you make in bus stations

a tape cassette of you and your friends together, talking and kidding around

a weekly menu from the school cafeteria

all the stuff that's in your pockets right now

ticket stubs from rock concerts, plays, events you've attended during the year

a TV guide

movie listings from the newspaper

letters you received during the year

some mail, including that junk

a road map showing the route of a trip you took recently, traced with a felt-tip pen

labels off of boxes, bottles, and cans of your favorite foods

birthday, get well, and Christmas cards from the past year

your favorite magazines and comics (or parts of them)

new recipes discovered during the year

Xerox makes time machines

Pictures are little time warps taking you into the past as far back as you would like to go. Photographs have recorded images of people, events, and places over the past hundred years or so; paintings and drawings did the same job for thousands of years before that. Pictures are a way of getting to know people and places that were long ago — far away places that cannot be any more.

Pictures make history fun, particularly backyard history, and we'll want to get lots of them. But how to do it? Old prints were separated from their negatives long ago. Daguerreotypes, tintypes, and polaroid pictures have no negatives from which to make more copies. Besides, all this photography, though fun, gets pretty complicated and expensive.

One way you can get dozens of images for 5¢ or 10¢ is with the Xerox magic time machine. Here's how to do it . . .

Arrange as many as you can on a piece of 8½x11 paper (regular writing paper). Put them close together so that you can get lots of pictures on each page.

Hold each picture down with a drop of rubber cement. It's important to use rubber cement because it won't hurt the picture and because it will hold the picture while you need it held down but won't hold it down forever.

Gather together all the pictures of friends, family, and places that you'd like to copy.

Have as many copies made as you want. The pictures may not be as distinct as those reprinted from negatives, but if your originals are pretty clear and the machine is working well (it might help if you tell the operator to make them extra dark) you'll get some nice pictures.

After you've got lots of pictures . . .   make a family history wall or bulletin board with images of your ancestors.

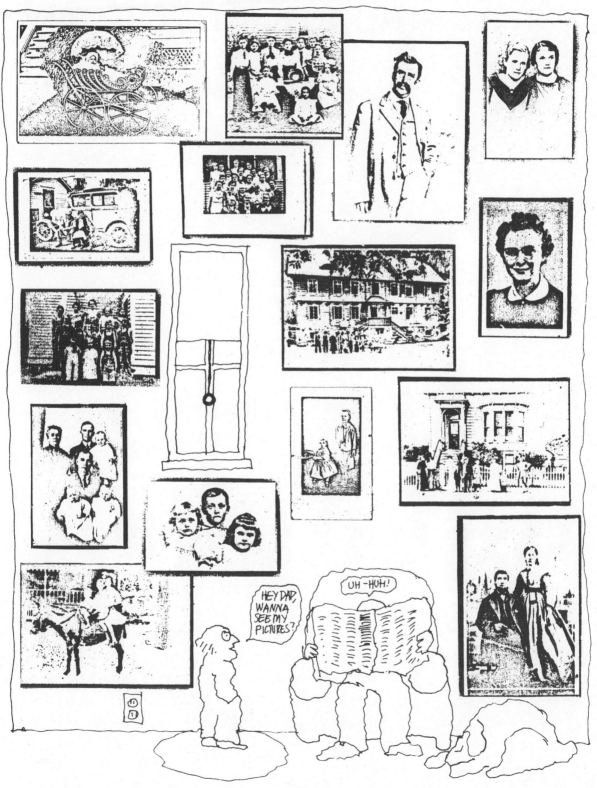

WOW
have you got ancestors!

Me

Mom   Dad

My grandparents

My great-grandparents

My great-great-grandparents

Feeling alone? Well, here's what five generations, or about the last 150 years of your family (anybody's family), looks like. It often happens these days that there are five generations of a family alive at one time, so this is how many people you'd have to invite to a family reunion (plus all your brothers and sisters, aunts and uncles, cousins, great-aunts and uncles — but we'll talk about that later).

How many relatives have you got, anyway?

Here's a way to help you visualize the size and shape of your family.

1. Make a rubber stamp ancestor by gluing a small piece of linoleum onto a block of wood and then cutting a figure on it,

or by cutting it on the end of an old eraser,

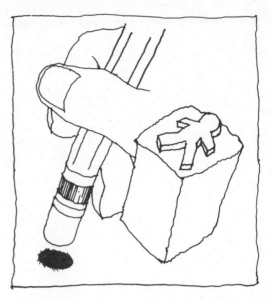

or just by using the eraser on a new pencil to make a small dot. (You'll see why they have to be small.)

---

2. Get a stamp pad,

3. And a piece of wrapping paper off a roll (like the kind you find in meat markets and produce stores). Get a l-o-n-g piece.

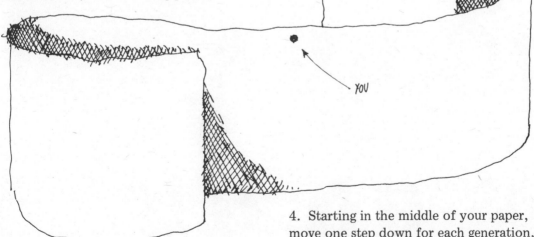

YOU

4. Starting in the middle of your paper, move one step down for each generation, showing the number of individuals in that generation. Put yourself at the top.

How many will there be in the fifth generation?

How many will there be in the tenth generation?

How many generations will you diagram before you give up?

You can also add birth dates to each generation to get some idea how far back in time you're going. A "generation" is usually defined as the number of years between the birth of the parents and the birth of their offspring. Of course this varies, so we'll have to guess at some average, like 25 years, which might look something like this . . .

MAKE YOUR GENERATION CHART AN ILLUSTRATED ONE! DRAW OR COLLECT A BUNCH OF PICTURES LIKE THIS — OBJECTS OR EVENTS WHICH ARE RIGHT FOR EACH GENERATION IN YOUR CHART. SEE IF ANY GROWN-UPS CAN THINK OF OTHERS. IF YOU CAN'T FIND PICTURES, JUST USE WORDS.

A family map

One of the things you've probably discovered from all this digging into the family past is that people have really moved around a lot, and are still moving. For Americans today it all began with that long trip from the "old country." Since then, later generations have moved from New York to Indianapolis, to Chicago, and St. Louis, and on to Phoenix and Los Angeles. An uncle in Little Rock, the two cousins who visited you last year from Des Moines, an aunt you've never met in Fargo, great-aunts and uncles, first and second cousins, scattered all over the place. You'll realize just how much moving about American families do, when you try to make a family map.

Buy an outline map of the United States showing state boundaries (I bet your teacher will give you one for free), or trace a map from an atlas.

Using dots to mark the cities, and lines to show movement, begin with your parents' birthplaces and trace their moves, through their childhoods and yours, up to today. It might be a fun after-dinner game. Get your mother and father thinking about all the places they've lived and put them down on your map.

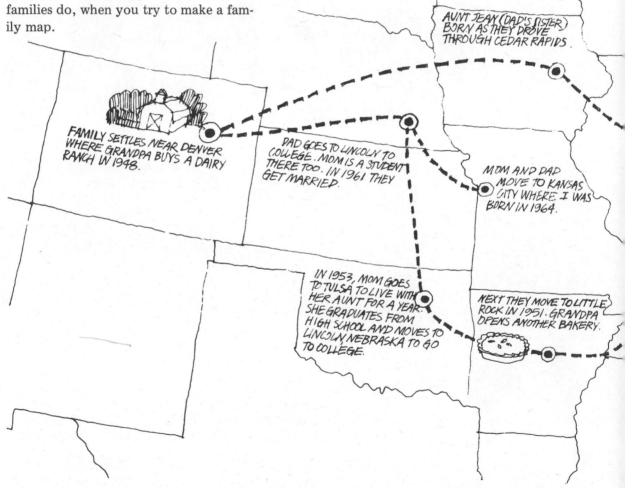

AUNT JEAN (DAD'S SISTER) BORN AS THEY DROVE THROUGH CEDAR RAPIDS.

FAMILY SETTLES NEAR DENVER WHERE GRANDPA BUYS A DAIRY RANCH IN 1948.

DAD GOES TO LINCOLN TO COLLEGE. MOM IS A STUDENT THERE TOO. IN 1961 THEY GET MARRIED.

MOM AND DAD MOVE TO KANSAS CITY WHERE I WAS BORN IN 1964.

IN 1953, MOM GOES TO TULSA TO LIVE WITH HER AUNT FOR A YEAR. SHE GRADUATES FROM HIGH SCHOOL AND MOVES TO LINCOLN, NEBRASKA TO GO TO COLLEGE.

NEXT THEY MOVE TO LITTLE ROCK IN 1951. GRANDPA OPENS ANOTHER BAKERY.

Then you might want to trace the geography of other generations: your grandparents, great-grandparents, even great-great-grandparents. For most of us this means making another map of somewhere else in the world, and going back beyond a port of entry like New York or San Francisco to some distant country.

You could also make a map showing where all your relatives are now. If your parents come from large families, this could turn out to be a real geography lesson.

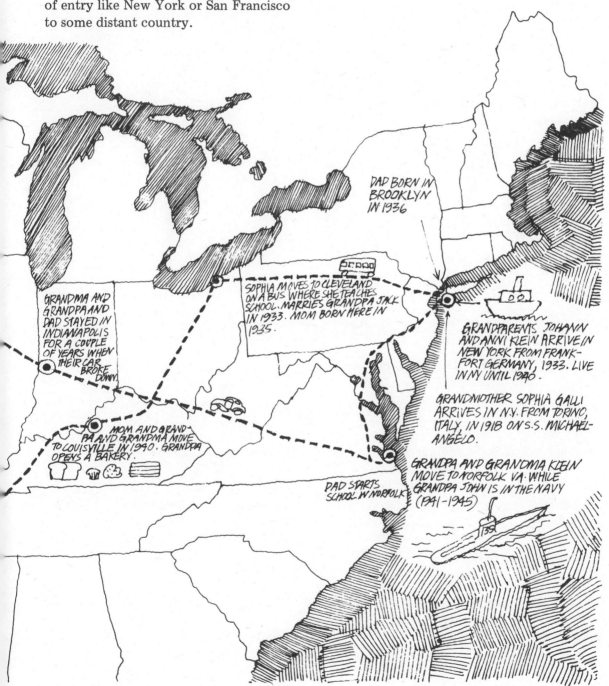

DAD BORN IN BROOKLYN IN 1936

GRANDMA AND GRANDPA AND DAD STAYED IN INDIANAPOLIS FOR A COUPLE OF YEARS WHEN THEIR CAR BROKE DOWN.

SOPHIA MOVES TO CLEVELAND ON A BUS WHERE SHE TEACHES SCHOOL. MARRIES GRANDPA JACK IN 1933. MOM BORN HERE IN 1935.

GRANDPARENTS JOHANN AND ANNI KLEIN ARRIVE IN NEW YORK FROM FRANKFORT GERMANY, 1933. LIVE IN NY UNTIL 1940.

GRANDMOTHER SOPHIA GALLI ARRIVES IN N.Y. FROM TORINO, ITALY, IN 1918 ON S.S. MICHAELANGELO.

MOM AND GRANDPA AND GRANDMA MOVE TO LOUISVILLE IN 1940. GRANDPA OPENS A BAKERY.

GRANDPA AND GRANDMA KLEIN MOVE TO NORFOLK VA. WHILE GRANDPA JOHN IS IN THE NAVY (1941-1945)

DAD STARTS SCHOOL IN NORFOLK

Out on a limb
of the family tree

Reading about the origins of names and counting your ancestors has probably raised more questions than answers (and that's good).

How do you know if your family name really can be traced back to a certain place? Or . . .

Did some distant ancestor actually do the kind of work your family name would suggest?

And what about your name, your first name? Where did it come from?

These questions lead to the next step along the way toward finding out who you are, by making a lineage chart or, more simply, a family tree. Like a tree, it has roots that show the main branches of your family, and looks like this:

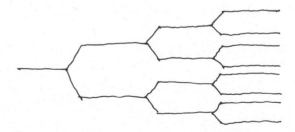

30

MAKE YOUR OWN FAMILY TREE BY COPYING THE CHART ON THIS PAGE
AND THE NEXT ONE ONTO A PIECE OF PAPER.

AS YOU MOVE ACROSS THE CHART THIS WAY YOU'RE MOVING BACK
IN TIME FROM THE PRESENT (YOU) TO YOUR PARENTS, AND SO ON:

Sherman Robinson

January 6, 1936
Muncie, Indiana

↑

DO THE SAME FOR YOUR
FATHER (NAME ON
TOP, PLACE AND DATE OF
BIRTH UNDERNEATH)

PUT YOUR NAME ON THE TOP OF
THIS FIRST LINE.

↓

Cynthia Robinson

November 3, 1962
Oakland, California

↑

AND THE DATE AND PLACE OF
YOUR BIRTH UNDERNEATH

AND FOR YOUR
MOM

↓

Mary Tolliver

April 13, 1937
Lafayette, Indiana

Andrew Robinson
June 1, 1890
Kirkcaldy, Scotland
AND YOUR GREATGRANDPARENTS

James Robinson
December 24, 1909
Chicago Illinois

*YOUR FATHER'S PARENTS
GO HERE
(YOUR GRANDPARENTS)*

Belle Jankes
August 12, 1892. New Haven, Connecticut

John Brooks
October 19, 189(?) St. Louis, Missouri
ON YOUR FATHER'S SIDE)

Veva Brooks
March 18, 1911
St. Louis, Missouri

Sarah Hunter
November 24, 1895
Poplar Bluff, Missouri

Abraham Tolliver
(?) Richmond or Bloomington (?)

AND YOUR GREATGRANDPARENTS

Walter Tolliver
July 23, 1912
Richmond, Indiana

*AND YOUR MOTHER'S
PARENTS HERE*

Ella Williams
May (?) 1894 or '95 (ask Grandma Tolliver) (?)

Joe Campbell
1890 Southampton, England

ON YOUR MOTHER'S SIDE

Edna Campbell
February 3, 1913
Indianapolis, Indiana

Lina Mae Haywood
August 4, 1898 Brooklyn, N.Y.

WHEW!

Hints for the Family Historian

Pick a relaxed, comfortable time with your parents to get into the past, maybe after dinner. Don't just ask and run, but explain what you're doing so they'll be interested too.

It takes a little time getting one's memory to reach back into the past, so don't expect answers right away. As people talk and begin focusing their minds on the past they'll also start remembering more and more.

Don't feel like you're intruding or wasting their time. Your mom and dad will enjoy your interest in their lives and, besides, it will give you something to talk about while you're all together.

Ask memory-jogging questions, like these:

Where were your mom and dad living when you were born?

Did your father fight in any wars? Where were they?

How old were you when I was born?

Did your father have a car when you were young? What's the first car you can remember riding in?

What was your favorite food when you were my age?

Did your mom and dad ever talk about their parents and grandparents?

How did it happen that you were born where you were?

Can you remember your first television set? What programs were on then?

How late did Grandma and Grandpa let you stay up to watch television?

Have you got any pictures of your parents? Grandparents? Great-grandparents?

How old was I when my grandfather (grandmother, great-grandfather, great-grandmother) died?

ANOTHER KIND OF TREE

With pictures you can make another kind of family tree which tells you not only who and when your ancestors were but also what they looked like. This is where family resemblances begin to show up. You can also discover a lot about the kind of clothes adults and children wore back then.

First of all, you'll need pictures. If you're lucky, your family will have a large collection of old photographs, some going back to the days of your great-great-grandparents, who were as intrigued by cameras and excited about having their pictures taken as you are. For them, it was a big event, so they put on their best clothes and most solemn expressions, and posed for posterity.

For your family portrait tree you'll want pictures in which the faces are large and fill the whole picture, or nearly so. Some of these faces will look pretty serious to you, even grim, but that was the fashion. And considering that people had to sit in front of the camera for a long time, sometimes with their head in a clamp to keep it still (because the first films took a long time to expose) it's a small wonder they weren't crying. Anyway, when the hand-held roll film camera came into being, people began having fun taking pictures, and it shows!

As you begin collecting pictures, you may discover some kinds that look really strange. You might find:

tintypes — positive photographs made on a thin iron plate enameled with a sensitized coating.

silhouettes — profile portraits cut out of black paper and pasted on a white or colored card.

ambrotypes — negative transparencies backed with black cloth or paint to make them look like positives.

oil paintings — usually done on canvas stretched on a wooden frame. Small paintings were often done on wood or board.

pen and ink sketches

glass plates — these are a wonder to look through and even more of a wonder if they've survived. Glass was used to make photographic negatives until flexible materials like celluloid and acetate were manufactured so that negatives could be made on sheets or rolls of film.

tinted photographs — photographs painted by hand in soft, pastel colors.

daguerreotypes — photographs made on a light-sensitive silver-coated metal plate. When you look straight at it you see a dim negative image, but turning it at an angle to the light a bright positive image suddenly appears.

calotypes — fuzzy, soft images printed from paper negatives.

Besides telling you something about the history of cameras and films, learning about the different kinds of early photographs also helps to date them. As each new process was invented it flourished for a while and then declined, being replaced by a newer, simpler, or better way. So if there is a picture with no date and disagreement among your family as to whether it's great-granddaddy or great-great-granddaddy, you'll be able to make a rough guess if you can identify the kind of picture it is.

Of course, several photographic processes were in use at any one time, so you can't be perfectly accurate. But you may be able to tell at least what generation the person's from.

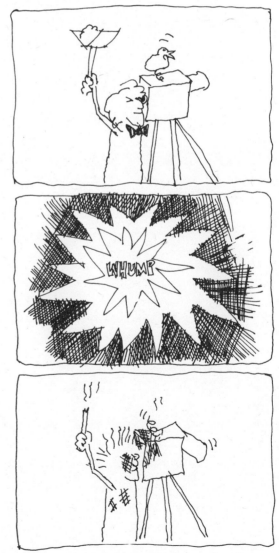

35

Some other clues:

Look for an embossed date in the paper or on the little folder with the photograph.

Compare clothing styles and hair styles with displays and mannequins in local museums, or with pictures in books.

If you know the birthdate of the person in the picture, try to guess their age at the time the picture was taken (anything goes).

Pass a copy of the picture around to older members of your family and ask them to guess at the date and write it on the back.

Some places where old pictures hide:

Unmarked boxes in attics and basements (all the more fun because you'll have to go through each box).

Tucked in old books, diaries, old school yearbooks, family Bibles (where you'll also find birth certificates).

Photo albums, and those yellow envelopes in which processed film and prints come back from the drugstore.

In the bottom of seldom used dresser or desk drawers.

1826 DAGUERREOTYPE
1839 CALOTYPE
1847 GLASS PLATES
1856 FIRST TINTYPES
1877 DRY GLASS PLATES
1888 KODAK'S FIRST PORTABLE ROLL FILM CAMERA
1900 KODAK'S FIRST BROWNIE CAMERA
1907 FIRST COLOR PHOTOS
1924 FIRST 35mm CAMERAS
1935 KODACHROME / KODACOLOR
1947 FIRST POLAROID
1950 FIRST XEROGRAPHY

WAIT! Be Careful with Those Old Photographs!

Photographs are a kind of historical document that requires very special care. Untold chapters of family history are lost because prints and, most important, negatives are not handled and stored properly. If you come across a large collection of old photographs, read these simple instructions *before going on.*

Handle negatives as little as possible. But when you must:

1. Wash your hands first. The oil on your fingers can leave permanent marks on a negative.

2. Touch only the edge or the very corner of a negative.

If you find a negative with someone's breakfast all over it, don't throw it away. Negatives can be cleaned. It's best to use the inexpensive cleaner available in small bottles at the camera store. But you can also clean negatives with alcohol and a cotton swab — carefully. Brush off dust and grit first, then gently wipe the negative, and wait for it to dry.

Negatives should be stored in envelopes.

Negative envelopes come in many sizes: 35 mm, 120, 4x5, 5x7, 8x10.

Watch out for glass plates. These are probably over a hundred years old! Put them in separate envelopes so that they can't rub together and store them so corners and edges don't get chipped. Even if a plate is cracked, save it; broken glass plates can still produce beautiful prints.

And be on the lookout for very old 35 mm nitrate film. Before the invention of modern acetate film, 35 mm films were made of a *highly inflammable* plastic which becomes kind of gooey when it gets very old. If you suspect you have some of this film, *don't* put it in your archives. Take it to an experienced photographer for identification. If what you have is nitrate base film, you can have it copied on new film (and it may look even better than the original print). If you have lots of this kind of film, take it to your local museum; they'll know how to handle it and can judge its historical value.

Keep all the negatives and prints you find until you've had a chance to go through them. They are all a valuable part of your family history.

Remember the backyard historian's motto:

IF IN DOUBT, KEEP IT!

Families come in all shapes and sizes

And to make sense of all these variations, anthropologists have thought up what's called a kinship chart. It's a way to arrange all your family around you on paper, so you can see who's who. It's also a way to answer questions like, What's a second cousin? or, How is a great-aunt related to me?

To make a kinship chart you first need to know a few simple symbols,

Female (mother, sister, aunt, grandmother)

Male (father, brother, uncle, grandfather)

Marriage

Line of descent

All of which together looks something like this:

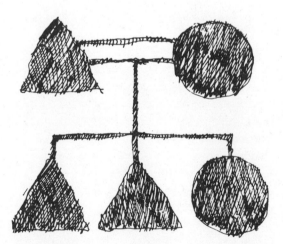

And here's how to make your own kinship chart:

1 PUT YOURSELF  OR
IN THE MIDDLE OF A BIG SPACE

2 ADD YOUR PARENTS

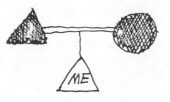

3 YOUR BROTHERS AND
SISTERS

4 AUNTS AND UNCLES

WAIT — THERE'S MORE...

5 AND YOUR GRANDPARENTS

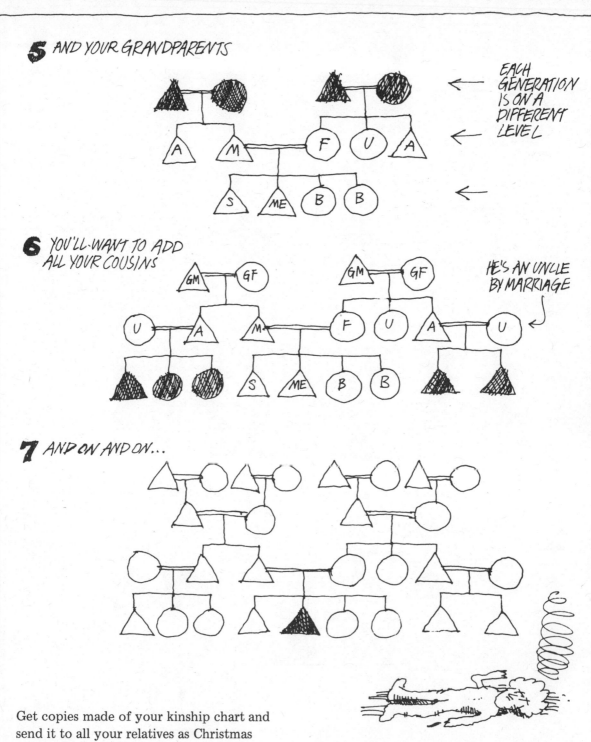

← EACH GENERATION IS ON A DIFFERENT LEVEL

←

←

6 YOU'LL WANT TO ADD ALL YOUR COUSINS

HE'S AN UNCLE BY MARRIAGE

7 AND ON AND ON...

Get copies made of your kinship chart and send it to all your relatives as Christmas cards/gifts. (Ask them to make a copy of it, fill in the blank spaces, add long lost cousins and new babies, and send it back to you.) This may be the beginning of a new family tradition!

If you make the circles and triangles big enough you can put pictures in them.

You'll probably want to put names and birthdays for each member of your family.

40

Eating your way through history

The next time you are visiting your grandparents, and the talk gets around to food or family (and it usually does), ask them what their favorite old recipes are. And which one is the oldest.

How old *is* it? Was it a recipe of their parents? Their grandparents? Their great-grandparents?

Collect as many old recipes as you can. If some of them are in the original handwriting (they could be up to a hundred years old!), make copies of them and add them to your family archives.

Try to get a name attached to each recipe.

Then make a family recipe book with the cook's picture on the page with his or her recipe.

Or, make family recipe calendars to be sent out as Christmas presents. Place the recipe, along with a picture of the grandparent, great-grandparent or great-great-grandparent to whom it belonged, on a sheet of paper with a calendar for the month (you can get free calendars lots of places). If possible, use copies of the original recipe card in order to preserve the handwriting.

Make as many copies of your family recipe calendar as you need, and you'll have the best old-fashioned presents ever.

Grandma Weitzman's Pumpkin Pie

OCTOBER

SUN	MON	TUE	WED	THU	FRI	SAT
•	•	•	1	2	3	4
5	6	7	8	9	10	11
12	13	14	15	16	17	18
19	20	21	22	23	24	25
26	27	28	29	30	31	•

Pop, mood and rock

How much do you know about your parents' younger days? For example, the music they listened to on the radio and the records they bought and danced to.

Well, ask them about the music they liked as teenagers, and ask them also if they have any of their old records around. Until the 1950's, records were bought mostly by adults. By the late 1950's teenagers were buying 70 percent of all the records made. These were the years your mom and dad were probably going through elementary and high school. And it was during this decade that rock-and-roll music began.

THE OLD DOG QUIZ OF POP MUSIC

HOW MUCH DO YOU KNOW ABOUT MUSIC FROM "THE OLD DAYS"? HOW MUCH DO GROWN UPS KNOW? SEE HOW MANY OF THESE QUESTIONS YOU CAN ANSWER. THEN ASK AN ADULT.

1. In 1951 a female singer recorded a song that became the greatest selling *single* up to that time. What is her name? What is the name of the song?

2. The term "rock-and-roll" came out of the fifties. Okay, where did it come from?

3. A black male singer recorded the first LP to sell a million copies. What is his name?

4. What grades were your mom and dad in when these songs were among the Top Ten? And who sang them?

Mona Lisa

Put Your Head on My Shoulder

Rock Around the Clock

Mockin' Bird Hill

All Shook Up

Cry

Great Pretender

You You You

Bird Dog

Sh-Boom

(Give bonus points if they can sing the opening lines of each song.)

SCORE YOURSELF

ONE POINT FOR EVERY RIGHT ANSWER (INCLUDING CORRECT FIRST LINES)

0-5 POINTS, A REAL DRAG

5-10 POINTS, NOT TOO HIP

10-15 POINTS GETTING THERE, DADDY-O

15-20 POINTS PRETTY HIP

(20 OR BETTER — FLIP-OUT CRAZY GONE!)

ANSWERS TO THE QUIZ ⇩

NO FAIR LOOKING AT THIS BOX UNTIL YOU'VE TRIED TO ANSWER THE QUESTIONS. NO PEEKING.

1. **Patti Page**/*Tennessee Waltz*

2. Disc jockey Alan Freed coined it from a line of an old blues song, "My baby rocks me with a steady roll."

3. **Harry Belafonte**

4.
- 1950/Nat King Cole
- 1951/Patti Page
- 1952/Johnnie Ray
- 1953/Ames Brothers
- 1954/Crew Cuts
- 1955/Bill Haley and the Comets
- 1956/The Platters
- 1957/Elvis Presley
- 1958/Everly Brothers
- 1959/Paul Anka

43

The mirrored image

Are you, your brother or sister, or your mom and dad into photography? Well if you are, even in a small way, and you have a 35mm camera, or a Polaroid, or a Kodak Instamatic, you're ready to do a super-professional job on your family history archives.

You may have hundreds of family pictures, but probably very few negatives (they're not as interesting as snap shots, so their survival chances are lower). So, if an old picture is lost or damaged, it's all over. With-

out a negative there's just no way to bring that picture back to life again. But if you learn how to make your own copy negatives, then not only can you make a new print, but you can also make it any size you want. And often the print you make will be better than the original.

If your archives are in good shape — with your family pictures arranged by subject, and each picture with the name of the person you got it from penciled on the back — you're ready to start. You'll need:

44

a work table (a folding card table will do) or a tripod,

some sunshine, or (if it's winter and you live in Alaska),

two lamps,

a piece of heavy posterboard, about 11x14 inches,

your camera and a copy attachment,

some film (Plus X or Verichrome),

a roll of masking tape,

and your collection of old pictures.

Here are some ways of setting up for copying:

YOUR CAMERA

YOU'LL NEED A CLOSE-UP ATTACHMENT — AN ACCESSORY WHICH FITS OVER THE LENS AND MAKES IT POSSIBLE TO GET CLOSE TO YOUR SUBJECT. THESE ARE AVAILABLE FOR MOST INEXPENSIVE CAMERAS LIKE POLAROIDS OR KODAK INSTA- MATICS.

SOME CAMERAS HAVE A PLACE FOR A WIRE ATTACHMENT LIKE THIS. THE WIRE IS USED WITH THE CLOSE-UP ATTACHMENT AND SHOWS HOW CLOSE YOU SHOULD GET TO THE SUBJECT AND WHAT YOUR CAMERA WILL "SEE".

FANCIER 35mm CAMERAS WITH REMOVABLE LENSES HAVE "EXTENSION TUBES" WHICH FIT BETWEEN CAMERA AND LENS AND ACT AS A CLOSE-UP ATTACHMENT.

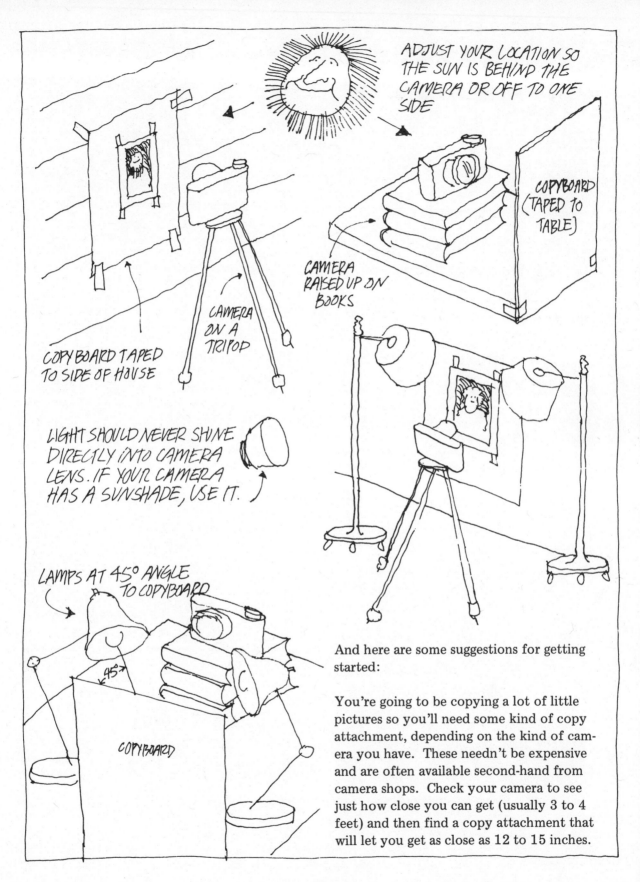

ADJUST YOUR LOCATION SO THE SUN IS BEHIND THE CAMERA OR OFF TO ONE SIDE

COPYBOARD (TAPED TO TABLE)

CAMERA RAISED UP ON BOOKS

CAMERA ON A TRIPOD

COPYBOARD TAPED TO SIDE OF HOUSE

LIGHT SHOULD NEVER SHINE DIRECTLY INTO CAMERA LENS. IF YOUR CAMERA HAS A SUNSHADE, USE IT.

LAMPS AT 45° ANGLE TO COPYBOARD

45°

COPYBOARD

And here are some suggestions for getting started:

You're going to be copying a lot of little pictures so you'll need some kind of copy attachment, depending on the kind of camera you have. These needn't be expensive and are often available second-hand from camera shops. Check your camera to see just how close you can get (usually 3 to 4 feet) and then find a copy attachment that will let you get as close as 12 to 15 inches.

If you don't have a light meter, try this experiment to find the best exposure for your camera and film.

1. Set up two 75-watt lamps about a foot and a half from the copyboard.

2. Put Plus X or Verichrome (the same as Plus X) in your camera. Set the lens at f8, and the shutter speed at 125th. (If your camera doesn't have adjustable shutter speeds and lens openings, it's probably set at this combination permanently, anyway.)

3. Take a picture. Then, using the *same* photograph,

4. Take another picture at a 60th, and then,

5. Take another picture at a 30th (leaving the lens set at f8 the whole time).

6. Do this again with the next photograph you are going to copy, and the next, until you finish that roll.

7. Have this first roll developed before you do any more copying. When the developed negatives come back, take a look at the three frames of each photograph you copied. One will look too dark. One will look too light. And one should be just right. Use *that* lens opening and shutter speed combination for all your pictures and you'll be OK most of the time. (You'll eventually learn from your black frames and washouts to make adjustments when they're necessary.)

If you're using a 35mm camera, buy 36-exposure rolls. This works out to a little more than 3 cents a picture.

PICTURE IS BADLY UNDER-EXPOSED. PRINT WILL BE VERY LIGHT.

THIS ONE IS JUST ABOUT RIGHT

THIS ONE IS TOO LIGHT— PICTURE WILL BE TOO DARK

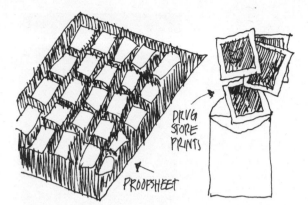

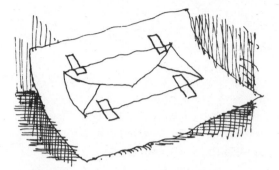

To keep negatives from going astray, put them in a letter envelope and glue or tape the envelope to the back of the proofsheet.

When you take your pictures to be developed (or if a friend is going to develop them for you) ask for an 8½″ by 11″ proofsheet. This will give you 36 or more little 1″x1½″ pictures. (If you are using larger film like 120, it's cheaper to get the little snapshots they give you as part of the developing deal.)

This is what your proofsheet will look like:

You can store your proofsheets in file boxes from your family archives, or you can punch three holes in them and put them in a three-ring binder, like this:

If you're collecting many family photographs, here's a simple way of organizing your copies:

Assign a letter (A, B, C, D, etc.) to each set of negatives and its proofsheet.

Then you can cut up the proofsheets and decide which of the little images you will want to use. (You might want to have two sets of proofsheets so you have one to cut up and one to tape your negatives to.)

48

Now you have lots of little pictures to work with. You could paste them on 4x6 index cards, making a card for your mom, another for your dad, another for your grandfather, and grandmother, and so on. Under each picture print the letter showing which proofsheet it's on and, if it helps, the frame number (E-12, A-26, and so on).

Then on the back of the card write down who the people are, the date of the photograph (if known), the place, the occasion (wedding anniversary, birthday, graduation) and any other bits of information that could so easily be lost.

As you can see, this whole thing is simpler and less expensive using 35mm film, but if your camera uses a larger film size you can design a filing system to fit your needs.

Oh yes, you'll need another shoebox for the family archives.

Hand-me-down history

As you begin collecting stories and images from the past you'll discover that an awful lot of history has been lost. Names, birthdays, exciting episodes, even whole families almost seem to have never existed, because they are lost to memory. Lost in crossing oceans. Lost in moving from town to town and from house to house. Lost when family members go their separate ways.

Perhaps you've already begun to wonder what's going to happen to your stuff, like favorite toys, school pictures, things you like to have around you, all those personal artifacts scattered about your room and your life. If so, you've probably been bitten by the family history bug.

Making a family history is not a day- or a week-long project. In fact, some people have spent their whole lives doing it. You probably won't finish it, but don't get discouraged. Just do a little at a time when you feel like doing it. As other people in your family discover what you're doing, they'll catch on too, and help you.

The important thing is not how long it takes or whether it ever gets finished, but that you begin now before things get lost.

Start right now getting all the bits and pieces of your family's past that are scattered about the house (or maybe several houses) into one place.

What kinds of things go into a history? Anything. Everything. At first you won't know what to keep and what not to, but after a while you'll develop a feeling for what is to be saved. There are no limits, but some of the things you ought to be on the lookout for are:

OBITUARY

Mrs. Sarah Mills Dies At 91 Years

Sarah Mills, who was born in 1842, passed away at the home of her daughter, Mrs. Carrie Stewart,

6 North Cleveland, this morning at 6:55 a.m., after an illness of five months. She was born at St. George, New Brunswick, 91 years and 10 months ago and is survived by two daughters, Mrs. Carrie Stewart, Wenatchee, and Mrs. Jennie Swan, Ore— Mrs. Bell—

FAMILY RECORD.

DEATHS

Page

High School

This Certifies That

DIPLO

51

images — photographs, drawings, portraits tucked away in the attic, newspaper clippings, home movies, drawings and things made at school, picture post cards, high school and college yearbooks, old magazines, medals and decorations, maps showing vacation routes, slogan buttons

copies of documents — birth certificates, business records, letters, school work (Remember how your parents kept those first spelling papers and math tests you brought home? Their parents did it too.), diaries, recipe cards, family bibles, death certificates, diplomas, wedding announcements, birth announcements, passports, wartime rationing coupons, old driver's licenses, military orders, birthday and Christmas cards, appointment calendars, shopping lists, bus, train, and plane tickets, musical comedy, theater, and concert programs, confirmation certificates, baptismal records

sounds — tape recordings, old phonograph records, player piano rolls, hit singles collected by your parents and grandparents, sheet music, wire recordings (used before tape), sound films

artifacts — old wedding gowns, baby shoes and clothes, quilts, needlework, furniture, jewelry, toys (your family might prefer that you use photographs of them for your collection)

And now, what to do with all this stuff.

Building Family Archives

You'll want to keep all this stuff organized and safe, so the first things you'll need are storage space and boxes.

The space for your family archives can be anywhere that's clean and dry. Closet shelves, filing cabinets, unused dresser drawers, underneath beds, cabinets, attic, garage, and basement storage space. Any place will do actually, but don't choose a place too far away or you'll forget about it. You'll want your archives within easy reach so that when the urge to work on them hits you they are available without a lot of hassle. And make sure everybody knows what you're doing so that the family archives don't disappear with the spring cleaning.

Then collect several sizes of boxes. Don't spend any money; they're all for free from local stores. Recycled shoe boxes are perfect for small photographs, color slides, and rolls of home movie film.

Copy services, printers, and stationery stores have large, sturdy boxes in which they receive reams of papers. These have removable lids instead of four flaps, they can be opened and closed easily, and they are dust proof. They are just right for storing old toys, your grandfather's baseball mit, that lace tablecloth from your great-grandmother's wedding chest, and your old teddy bear. Bigger boxes will also hold smaller boxes of pictures and letters. The kind of boxes oranges and apples now come in are good too.

And you'll need envelopes for little things: tiny photographs, the identification bracelet you got when you were born, and those comic buttons your dad and mom collected as kids. You can use recycled letter envelopes and large manila mailing envelopes, especially those with the clasps still working. Local stores or the place where your mom or dad works will be happy if you'll take this kind of stuff off their hands.

If you've got large photographs, old maps, posters, or other things too big to be put in boxes and envelopes without folding them thirty times, you'll want a couple of cardboard mailing tubes.

Getting Organized

Here's the hard part and the most important part, but also the most fun part, because you get to sort through all the things you've collected.

There's no right or wrong way to do it. Any system that keeps things in order and makes it easy to add new items as they are uncovered is fine. To start with, you might try this.

Develop a little code that can be penciled on the backs of things.

(Borrowing things brings with it some responsibilities, the most important of which is to know what belongs to whom. A code system will tell you who things belong to, no matter how much you shuffle them around.)

Make an envelope for each member of the family by placing their name in the upper left-hand corner (that's so you can thumb through them in their storage box and find the name you want). Then put them into a box in alphabetical order, so that your storage file looks something like this:

Keep your file handy and portable so that you can take it out in the evening after dinner and go over it with your mom and dad, or take it to family gatherings. But if you end up with hundreds of pictures, you may need to have several envelopes for each person, something like this:

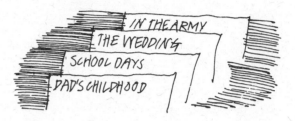

And don't forget an envelope for the family "mysteries," faces and places no one can remember. "How'd that picture get in there? That's not our family," or "You'll have to ask your grandmother about that one," are the pictures that end up in the envelope of family mysteries.

Then when the family's all together sometime, just get out your mystery envelope and start a "game" that could go all night, called "Who on earth could that be?" (You might talk your mom and dad into having special prizes for anyone who identifies a mystery ancestor.)

Here are some things you might do with your archives:

When your parents or grandparents have a big wedding anniversary celebration, surprise them with a history wall, a whole wall covered with photographs of their lives together.

At the next birthday party, put on display a whole bunch of pictures from the birthday person's childhood (your great-grandmother at the age of two on a bear skin rug). They probably haven't seen them for years, if ever.

Use copies of your oldest pictures as Christmas cards. You can even have postcard-sized prints made with a postcard form on the back, so you can just send them through the mail. (You can do this yourself if you or someone you know are into photography.)

Send picture cards to your relatives announcing the opening of your family archives. Tell them that if they'll send you copies of their old pictures for your files, you'll provide a picture-searching service, finding pictures they want of themselves or others they've never seen.

Make picture stories on special themes like:

Five Generations of Williamson Babies

Family Soldiers

Sports Greats of the Carter Clan

Houses We've Lived In

Traveling with the Tates

Styles of the Forties

All Our Pets

Automobiles in Our Past

Can You Name These Famous People?

Aunt Jean before Her Diet

1920's School Days

Use your experience as a family historian to help your friends get started on their own family histories.

As a school social studies project, keep your class up-to-date on the progress of your family history. Suggest to your teachers that credit be given for family history projects, and get other kids started.

History that talks

Those little cassette tape recorders everybody's carrying around these days not only let you record your favorite music but they're the historian's newest tool, particularly the family historian. There's just no way that you can collect "people history" as well as you can with a tape recorder. The recorded voice retelling an event is exciting and real in a way no written account can possibly be.

All you need is an inexpensive tape recorder (your own or borrowed), some tape cassettes, and an extra storage box in your family archives, and you're ready for some of the most exciting history you can imagine.

If you're bashful about using the recorder, try this for an opener. The next time you visit your grandparents for one of those long evenings of dinner and talk, take your tape recorder and a bunch of old pictures of your grandparents and your parents when they were young.

Tell them about your history project and that you've got a bunch of pictures you'd like them to see.

Pass out the pictures (you know, the one of your grandfather standing next to his new 1938 Chevy, or your grandmother's high school graduation).

Turn on your tape recorder.

Two hours later they'll still be laughing about how your grandfather lost the keys to the Chevy the night your mom was born, and you'll discover for the first time that she was actually born in a streetcar between Halstead and Grand. Or they'll tell you all about gas rationing during the war. Or about your dad's sixteenth birthday when he went to take his driving test. And on and on.

Want to try it? Here are some hints for success . . .

Don't set up formal "recording sessions"; this really turns people off. Take advantage of the light spirit and talkativeness of people at family reunions, Christmas dinners, and birthday parties, or just an evening with your folks.

Use the kind of tape recorder that has a built-in microphone. (Most of them come that way now.) Then you don't have machinery and wires out in the open scaring people. You don't have to hide the recorder, just keep it next to you on the couch or table. Most of the new microphones will pick up sounds anywhere in the room, but you should sit somewhere in the middle.

Use long tapes that last 90 or even 120 minutes.

Use pictures to get conversation started, but you might think of some questions to ask, too, like these:

If the talk of the evening centers around your pictures, keep a pencil handy to jot down names, dates, locations, and occasions on the backs of photographs.

Get as much from the talk as you can. If someone mentions a song they used to sing as a kid, ask them to sing it. If they talk about a thing that was important to them, ask if they still have it and if you can see it. Bringing out a favorite picture, or an old dress, or something your grandfather saved that belonged to his father gets minds going further and further into the past and starts whole new chapters in the history of you and your family.

Finally, when the evening's about to end or just after you get home, write on the label of the cassette the date, who was there, where it was, and, if it was special, the occasion.

Grandfathers and grandmothers don't last forever; some day you and your family will really enjoy getting that evening's tape out of your archives.

Friday night at Grandma's

Have you ever wondered about the things you and your family do in a certain way? How come it's always done *that* way? Like dinner at your grandmother's every Friday night. Or those plates that come down off the top shelf of the cupboard only on Christmas day. How about the chores that are passed down to the youngest son or youngest daughter? Or the Fourth of July house-cleaning and yard sale?

These are probably family traditions, things your mother and father did as children, and their mothers and fathers before them.

Some old traditions are very much alive, but the memory of why they're done in those particular ways has probably been lost somewhere. Other traditions, from earlier days, are lost entirely except perhaps in the memories of older folks. But as family historian, your task will be to find out about some of them and maybe even to get them going again.

Family life, in the days of your grandparents and great-grandparents, was strictly governed by tradition. This actually made things simpler, and wasn't as much of a burden as it might sound at first.

Raising a family is hard work, and for generations many parents found raising their kids the way they were raised, doing things the way their own moms and dads did them, just seemed to make good sense. That's tradition.

Traditions like special holiday dishes or Sunday family picnics, repeated year after year, gave each child and adult a sense of family time.

As children grew up and moved away to different cities, the Christmas dinner made sure that at least once a year there was a family again. And it made sure that new members of the family knew who their folks were.

Special chores for kids of different ages gave even the youngest child a role. Jobs like setting the table, going out for the Sunday paper, giving the dog his weekly bath, or helping younger sisters and brothers with homework gave everyone a part in the family's day-to-day life. Traditions made certain no one was left out.

Traditions gave each member a sense of place. You learned names for the other members of your family which helped you understand who they were and what they were to you, like Grandpa Joe, or Uncle Jim, or Cousin Beth, or Aunt Martha.

And tradition set rules for giving names to new babies.

So, get your tape recorder or note pad and find out all about your family traditions.

Ask your mom and dad about those special days and family ways of doing things.

Ask your grandparents about things they did as children. Do they still do them?

Why are certain dishes, or photographs, or pieces of furniture, or names, so important in your family?

Oh yes, and while you're at it, why not suggest that this Friday night you have dinner at Grandma's. It's been a long time, and she'll be happy to see you all again.

Clark Kent, decoder rings, and Ovaltine

OR I MIGHT BECOME A DRIFTER... A PANHANDLER WHOM NO ONE WOULD EVER SUSPECT OF BEING THE MAN OF STEEL!

Talking to older people about their past lives can get pretty fascinating, and very confusing. A lot of things they reminisce about and chuckle over will seem like a private joke to you. But, of course, you weren't around then and those things didn't affect your life as they did the people that lived through them. More wars than you can keep track of. That "Depression" your grandfather talks about. Your grandmother's stories about "rationing" and having enough "coupon books" to get the two pairs of shoes your dad went through every month. And those cars they refer to: "Nash" and "Hudson" and "DeSoto," "Edsels" and "Packards." It probably all seems like another world to you. But what's it all about?

Well, your mom and dad and your grand-parents are using words that aren't used much any more, talking about things that are no longer made, or radio programs that were their favorites before television arrived. It will happen with your children, too. You'll start talking someday about "rock bands" and "bikes" and they'll look at you as though you're speaking another language. What was important to you as a kid, just won't be important to them. That's a strange feeling, but that's how your parents probably feel.

If you'd like to understand their past a little better, there's a way to find out about the world as it was during the "fifties," or the "forties," or the "Great War," and it's as close and as simple as the library.

Old newspapers used to be bound together in heavy, clumsy volumes for storage, but you're in for a surprise today when you ask the librarian for some newspapers from the twenties or thirties. She'll bring you a little box containing a roll of film, point out a machine in the corner that looks like a TV set, and show you how to use a microfilm reader. Then, by simply turning a crank you can bring page after page of wondrous things before your eyes. By adjusting the microfilm reader one way you can scan whole pages, or with another adjustment zoom in on:

THE HIT PARADE

BLOCKBUSTER

rumble seat

Wedgies

food ads (Wow, look at those prices!)

fashion news (long dresses and broad shoulders, big lapels and baggy pants)

cars (the kinds you only see in museums now)

pictures of downtown (a traffic jam of horses and carts)

new houses (you might discover when your house was built)

news from abroad (Hey, I thought they had always been our friends!)

travel (now you know what the "Super Chief" and the "Twentieth Century Limited" are)

the first airplanes (often spelled "aeroplanes," they had only two motors, and little wheels in the back)

the radio log (*Allen's Alley*, *Gangbusters*, *Stella Dallas*, *One Man's Family*, *Captain Midnight*, *Ma Perkins*, *Terry and the Pirates*, *Inner Sanctum*, and more)

the movie section (*Gone with the Wind*, Betty Davis, Keystone Cops)

early TV programs (started about 1948 in larger eastern cities. For others, see papers from the early fifties)

sports (well, you don't need any help here)

comics (look for some that aren't around any more)

How'd they say it?

Your parents gettin' on your case about your jive? Well, the next time that happens, ask them how they would say it or, better yet, how they used to say it when they were your age. Your mom and dad are probably using your kind of language these days, but they used to have their own way of saying it, and you may be surprised that even twenty or thirty years ago some of your words would have been "in" — though you might discover a little difference in meaning and emphasis.

Make a list of the slang used by your parents and your grandparents as children. You might discover a "right on" expression that you can try out on your friends at school, and wouldn't that be the "cat's meow!"

Group your list of words by generation or by the decade in which they were "in" (1920's, 1950's). Have any of them survived or reappeared?

Listen carefully as the older members of your family talk about slang and you might discover some regional differences. (Do New Yorkers say it like they do in Chicago?) Some slang expressions are so local that you and other members of your family may never have heard them before.

Keep your list on a card in your family archives and add to it as more slang expressions are remembered. Make a list for your and your friends' slang expressions too — they go in and out of style pretty fast these days.

63

If you're fortunate enough to have at least one set of grand-parents who have lived for a long, long time in one place, you are in for a real adventure, because you get to play

Thingamajig

What's that? Well, a thingamajig is like a whatchimacallit or a thingamabob. You don't know its name or what it is used for. For example, this is a thingamajig . . . .

All right, let's try another one. This ought to be much easier, because you can see it in use . . . .

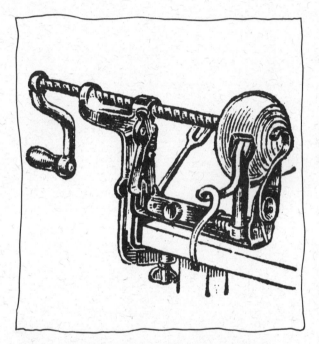

Any ideas?

No, it's not a pile of rusty tractor parts.

Wrong again, it's not the wreckage of a helicopter. Here's a hint: it was a common item in any kitchen, say, sixty years ago.

Give up?

It's a press used to extract juice from fruits and vegetables, and your great-grandmother probably had one because she also used it to make baby food.

Right! An apple peeler. And it's about the same age as that other thingamajig, that press, above. You're getting good at this.

Think you're ready to play THINGAMAJIG? All right, here's how to play.

First, you have to know where to look. Thingamajigs hang out in places like attics, cellars, garages, and storage sheds. Or some-times they're discarded in piles around farm buildings, or w-a-a-a-y in the back of unused kitchen cabinets (the one under the sink's a good bet).

64

Here's a test to find out just how good a
thingamajig hunter you are . . .

CAN YOU GUESS WHAT THESE ARE?
(ANSWERS ON PAGE 67)

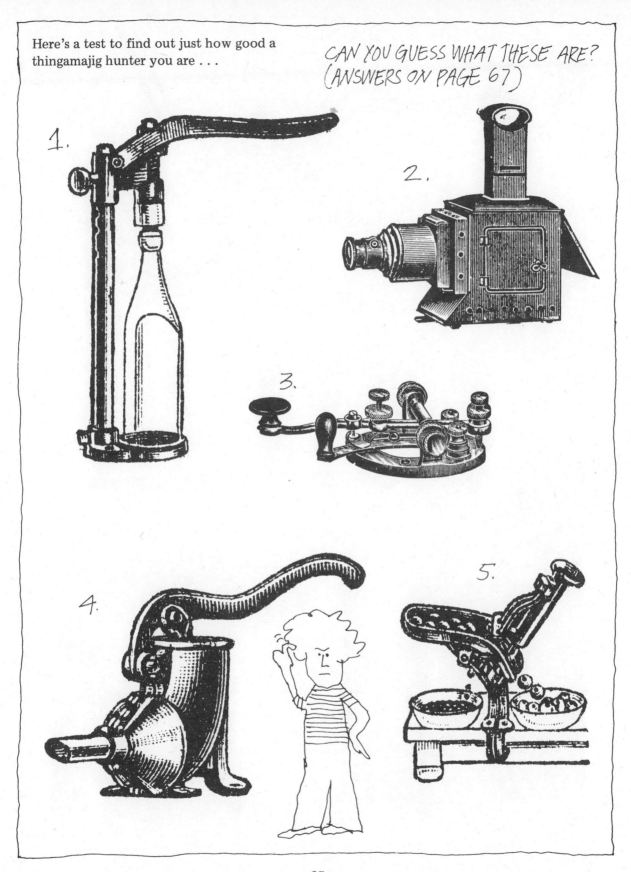

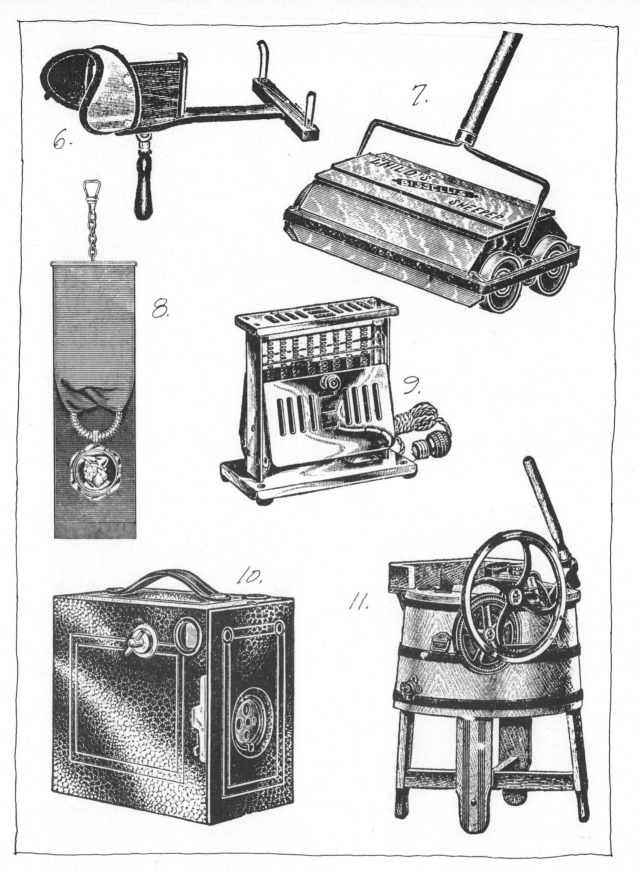

6.

7.

8.

9.

10.

11.

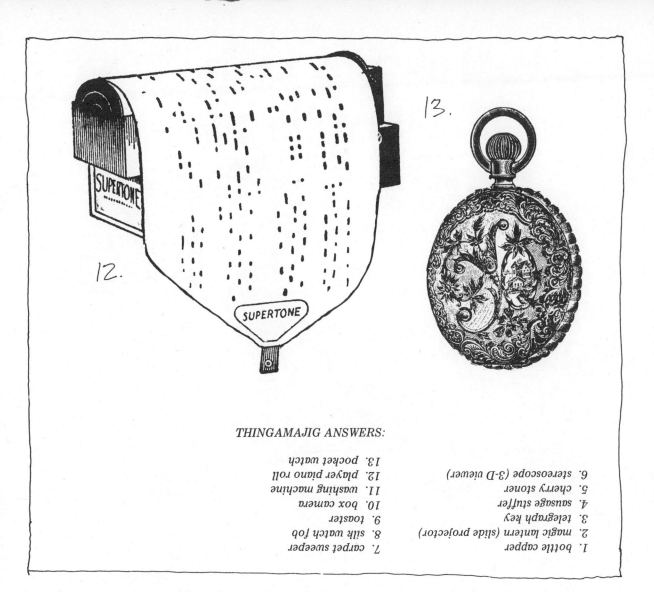

12.

13.

THINGAMAJIG ANSWERS:

1. bottle capper
2. magic lantern (slide projector)
3. telegraph key
4. sausage stuffer
5. cherry stoner
6. stereoscope (3-D viewer)
7. carpet sweeper
8. silk watch fob
9. toaster
10. box camera
11. washing machine
12. player piano roll
13. pocket watch

After you've found one, you have to guess what it is and how it was used. (No fair asking until you've really tried.)

Look closely for clues. Sometimes it says right on the thingamajig what it's for. Sometimes you can figure out how it was used by putting it together, or by turning its handles and watching how the parts move. Sometimes you can tell about how old it is if there's a patent date on it somewhere ("Pat. Pending" or "Patent no. ____" and then a date).

And sometimes, no matter how hard you try, you just can't guess what it is. That's the time to dust it off, put it out where everyone can see it and . . .

Invite the rest of the family to play THINGAMAJIG.

[By the way, never throw away a genuine, authentic thingamajig. If you don't want it anymore there are museums all over the country collecting thingamajigs (and thingamabobs, too) and any one of them might like to have it.]

History in the yellow pages

HIGHEST
PRICES PAID
ANTIQUE FURNITURE
TIFFANY, GLASS, CHIN
PAINTINGS - SILVER
PERSIAN RUGS

P. G. PUGSLEY & SON
On
Victorian Oak Office Furniture
And
Antique
Home Accessories

So Come In And
Browse And
Take An

BROWN'S ANTIQUE SHOP
FINE FURNITURE
PAINTINGS
COLLECTOR ITEMS
1211 Sutter --------------775-0800

THE JAZZ DISK
We buy, trade and sell
Jazz LP's
Noon — 7 p.m.
Tues.-Sat.
Closed Sunday
& Monday

3738
(at th
731-220

Antiques
LIZING IN OAK
FURNITURE
OSTALGIA
TEMS

18th & 19th CENTURY
FRENCH – ENGLISH – AMERICAN
FURNITURE & ACCESSORIES
Also
MARINE ANTIQUES
Antiques Purchased for Cash
Single Items & Estates
Hours 11 AM to 5:30 PM

TELEPHONE

If you have no big houses with cellars and attics for playing THINGAMAJIG, don't despair, there are special "museums" where thingamajigs also hang out, not at all like the museums you're used to.

Thingamajig museums have intriguing names like *The Attic* (there's a clue right there), *Grab Bag, Marta's Treasure House, Old Stuff, Repeat Performance, Salvation Army, Grandma's House, The Past Tense, Thrift Shop, Second Time Around, Yesterday's House, Antiques, Oddities & Monstrosities*, or very proper-sounding ones like *P. G. Pugsley & Sons* (specializing in Victorian office furniture). Unlike most museums, these are not cold, imposing structures a long bus ride away, but little places scattered about the town in store fronts and old houses. The exhibits change frequently (they must, or the "museum" goes out of business) and you can visit them week after week, even daily, and find still more things from the past. These are antique shops, junk yards, second-hand and resale shops, and there are probably several right in your neighborhood.

Best of all, the guide to finding all this stuff is right there in your own house, in the telephone book! Just look in the Yellow Pages under *Antiques — Dealers, Antiques — Repairing and Restoring*, or *Second-hand Dealers*.

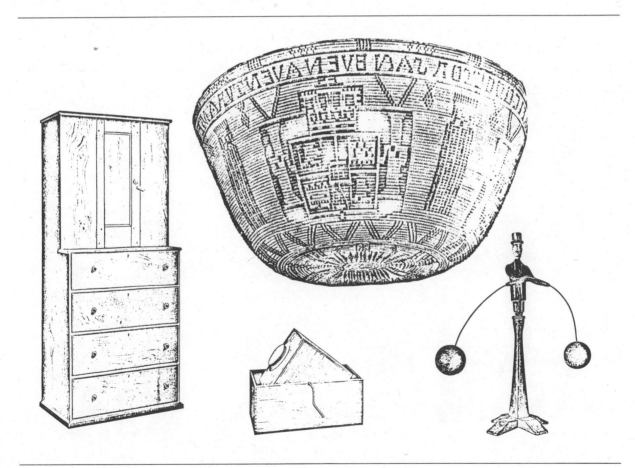

Antique dealers, of course, are in business to make money, so they're not really public museums. Still, you shouldn't be afraid to go in and just look around. Dealers are used to people "just looking." And most dealers are friendly people, glad to talk to you about the things they have. Besides, they know a lot about history and are quite experienced at playing the THING-AMAJIG game.

At first the array of old stuff will seem pretty confusing. There is seldom much order or reason to it all, but with a little experience you'll soon be able to spot items from a particular period, notice the different kinds of wood and metals, like tin and bronze, which aren't used much any more, and get a real sense of the past.

After a while you can play the THINGA-MAJIG game with a new slant, looking for things from certain times or from a special part of the country. But here's a real test for the thingamajig hunter.

How many of these things can you find?

a bicycle from the 1800's

toys from the time of your mother's and father's childhood

an automobile license plate from the 1920's

clothing worn in the time of your great-grandparents

the issue of *Life* magazine for the week you were born (If you find it, buy it; it's probably only 50¢ or so and well worth it.)

records and sheet music of your parents' favorite old songs

a TV set from the late 1940's

movie posters from the days of silent films

a *National Geographic* with an article about your town twenty or thirty years ago

Because we Americans move around a lot (how many places were on your family map?) it is unlikely that many of the things in your town's antique and second-hand stores came from the community. Whether they're homemade originals or mass-produced, they are a real part of America's past, and if they could talk, they'd have fascinating stories to tell about the people who have owned them and the places they've been.

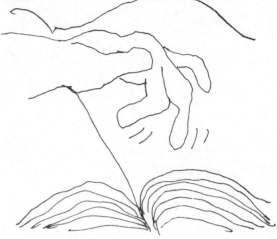

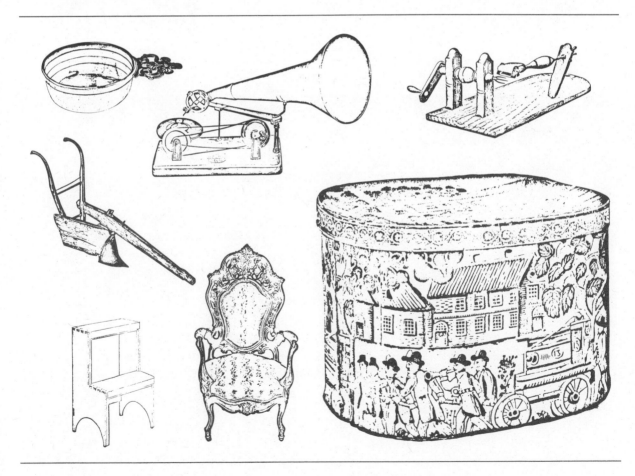

History at the cemetery

That's right, the cemetery. That's where you're going today.

No, it's not scary there.

What? No, there aren't any ghosts and vampires, but there's a lot of backyard history to be found in a cemetery. Some of your own personal history too, if any of your ancestors are buried there.

Afraid of going alone? You can take a friend . . . yes, a big friend's all right . . . but you may find you won't be alone at all at the cemetery.

Here's why. In a special survey some people spent a lot of time observing and talking to folks visiting cemeteries in the Boston area. They found that most of the people (726) were there, as you might expect, to visit family gravesites. But almost as many people (657) were making historic gravesite visits. Others came just for a walk, to play games, to pick berries, to make stone rubbings, and to photograph historic tombstones.

So there, you see, you won't be alone. There'll be lots of backyard historians to keep you company.

What are you supposed to do when you get there?

Visit the graves of your ancestors if any are buried there. It's a good time to check out the dates you need for your family tree. You'll also find out the maiden names of some of the women way back in your family's past.

Often, there is engraved on the stone a favorite saying, or poem, or picture. There's a tombstone of an old railroad man, in an Arkansas cemetery, that has a photograph of his 1880's steam locomotive under a little oval of glass right there at the top of his stone. His tombstone also carries information about his run. (Railroad men used to spend much of their lives on one preferred run.)

Some tombstones list the person's children.

Tombstones of soldiers tell about the battles and wars they fought in and, perhaps, died in.

The large number of children's tombstones from the 1800's tells us something about how hard it was to survive then.

Large numbers of tombstones from the same year or two often reveal epidemics in the past. If many of the stones have the same date on them, checking the newspaper for that day might show that there was some kind of catastrophe, like a flash flood, a tornado, or big accident.

Cemeteries can also serve as a kind of census of a town for a certain period, telling us

something about the nationalities, occupations, and family patterns of the people who first settled there. They also tell us when large numbers of immigrants from a certain country arrived in the locale.

For the artist, photographer, or backyard historian given to collecting rubbings, there is a tremendous variety of early American art available in a cemetery. (Take a look at the section in this book on how to make a rubbing.)

So, see how many things about your town and its people you can find while spending a sunny afternoon at the cemetery.

At the corner of Yolo and Poonkinney

Standing at a corner waiting for the light to change? Well, use your minute and a half to look around at the street signs on each corner, and discover some more back-yard history.

Never thought much about street names, have you? Well, if you traveled a lot from city to city in different parts of the country you'd realize that much of the flavor, and spirit, and history of a town is right there in those little street signs.

So what can you learn from street signs? The origins of the people who first settled your town, for one thing. In the southwest and in California, for example, you'll find a lot of towns and streets with Spanish names. That's because this area of the country once belonged to Mexico. The names of streets in New Orleans — Beaucaire, Chantilly, Lafitte, Montpelier, Rocheblave, Seine — attest to that city's French origins. In Chicago there is a Pulaski Road, named by the Polish community for their countryman who was a hero of the American Revolution.

And the names of the native American tribes which settled the area your town is in, for another. The names of chiefs and the Indian words for rivers, mountains, and other geographical features also became street names in many places.

On street signs you'll often find the names of well-known members of the community throughout its history. Mayors, city councilmen, police and fire heroes, writers and artists, and the names of other famous people from your town are probably also on street signs somewhere. If your address is on L'Enfant Drive in the District of Columbia, you probably know that your street was named for the French engineer who designed the city.

The light's changed, so you'd better go on now. If you're interested in the origins of the name of the street you're on right now or the one you live on, stop at the city clerk's office. They'll have the answer there or be able to refer you to someone who does.

1890's auction: a history game

At the next family get-together, or when you're with a group of friends, or even with your class in school, have a pretend auction of articles from your great-grandparents' day.

You'll be the auctioneer. And here are the rules of the game:

First, what you're going to sell at your auction are these items from the 1897 Sears, Roebuck catalog. Your job is to show your audience the item and read them the description from the catalog (the prices are on page 80, so they can't see them). Give them a real sales pitch.

After everyone's had a chance to look at the article closely, start the bidding. The object is to buy the item at the original price, the price at which it was offered for sale in the catalog.

After all the bids are in (you can write everybody's name on a blackboard or large piece of paper with their bid after their name), you "sell" the item to the bidder who came closest to the actual price in 1897.

Sell all the items shown here and add up the number of items each player has "bought." The player who "buys" the most items wins.

If you really like the game and want to play it again with the same people or need more items to auction off, you can get more items to sell from copies of *The Sears, Roebuck Catalog* in the library or from magazine and newspaper ads from any period you choose. In this way you could have a "birthday auction" for someone in your family with items taken from magazine and newspaper ads appearing on the day of their birth or some particular day of their life.

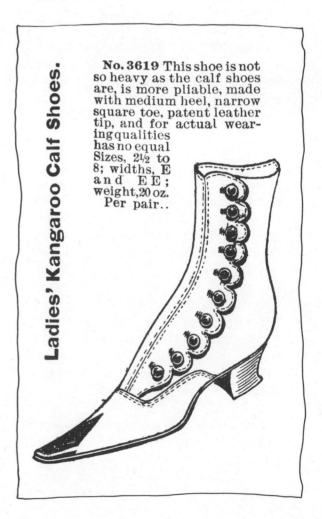

Ladies' Kangaroo Calf Shoes.

No. 3619 This shoe is not so heavy as the calf shoes are, is more pliable, made with medium heel, narrow square toe, patent leather tip, and for actual wearing qualities has no equal Sizes, 2½ to 8; widths, E and EE; weight, 20 oz. Per pair..

GENERAL DESCRIPTION.

BODY—The frame of the body is made of the best seasoned white ash, mortised, glued and screwed. **THE PANELS** and **SEATS** are made of the best seasoned poplar, all screwed, plugged and glued. **THE SILL** is rabbeted out and the floor sets in this rabbett, letting the floor down even and flush with top sill. **THE STEP BAR** is of seasoned oak and gained in the sill from the under side, making it impossible to break through the bottom when putting your weight on the step. Has full length Norway iron **BODY LOOPS**, 6 inch **RUB IRONS. THE BODY** is 52 inches long, 22 inches wide at bottom, 23 inches at top. **PANELS**, 8 inches deep. Made with two braces to the panel inside in addition to the seat frame brace. **SEAT** is 27 inches wide at the bottom, 15 inches deep, and 38½ inches to top of seat panel. **SEAT PANEL is** 26 inches deep, 11 inches from the floor to the bottom of seat and 15 inches from the floor to the top of cushion. **THE SEAT** is held to the body by two wrought iron seat rods going through the sills. Distance from top of cushion to roof of top, 39 inches; inside measurement 37 inches; between the bows at top is 44 inches.

We can furnish any of these rigs in three-fourths size when desired, making the **BODY** 19 inches wide at the bottom and 20 inches at the top; **SEAT** 24 inches at bottom and 34½ inches at top. Height of back, depth of panels, length of top, distance between top cushions and roof are the same as the regular sized buggy, and constructed in the same substantial and workmanlike manner.

GEARS—These buggies have our regular 15-16 inch double collar, best **STEEL AXLE** with a graceful downward sweep; **HICKORY AXLE CAPS** closely fitted to the axle, double perch of best hickory with steel plates running the entire length. **THE GEAR** is substantially braced by wrought iron stays running from perch to rear axle. We use the full back circle fifth wheel, the best known to the carriage trade, with king bolt back of axle. The **SPRING BARS** are of good hickory with handsome scroll cut on the ends.

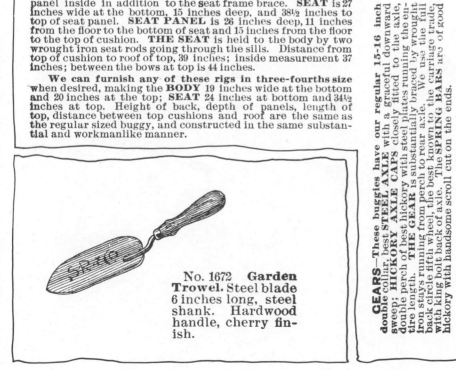

No. 1672 **Garden Trowel.** Steel blade 6 inches long, steel shank. Hardwood handle, cherry finish.

These suits run in sizes from 3 to 10 years of age. Be sure to state age of boy and whether large or small of his age. **No. 4185. TWO-PIECE SAILOR SUIT.** Wash goods, consisting of one light blue sailor blouse and one pair of knee pants. This suit is made of striped pique, warranted fast color. It is good weight and a good wearing material, nicely made with large, square back sailor collar, lapel front. Collar, cuffs and lapel made of plain blue pique to match stripe in the garment. Collar and cuffs trimmed with two rows of fairy stitch braid, one outside pocket in blouse, with ivory buttons. Each suit is furnished with a whistle and cord. Price, per suit,

Ladies' Skates.

No. 14648. Ladies' Club Skate, with rolled cast steel polished runners, bright steel toe and heel plates, russet leather straps. Size, from 7 to 10 inches. Always give sizes in inches when ordering. Price per pair......

No. 783. A most amazing offer. **The violin** is a beautiful model, with name carved in scroll, and very fancy inlaying in back. The instrument is one that will attract the interest of professionals, on account of its beautiful full, round tones, as well as the richness of the finish and desirability of model. Full ebony trimmed. Reddish-brown color. We include a **violin bow** of decided excellence, it being made of Brazil wood. Round stick, with rounded ebony frog, German silver lined, fancy German silver button, pearl eye and pearl slide. The **fine wood violin case** is exposition shape, black varnished, full lined with flannel, with handle, lock and clasps. The **full set of strings** is of the most select superfine quality.

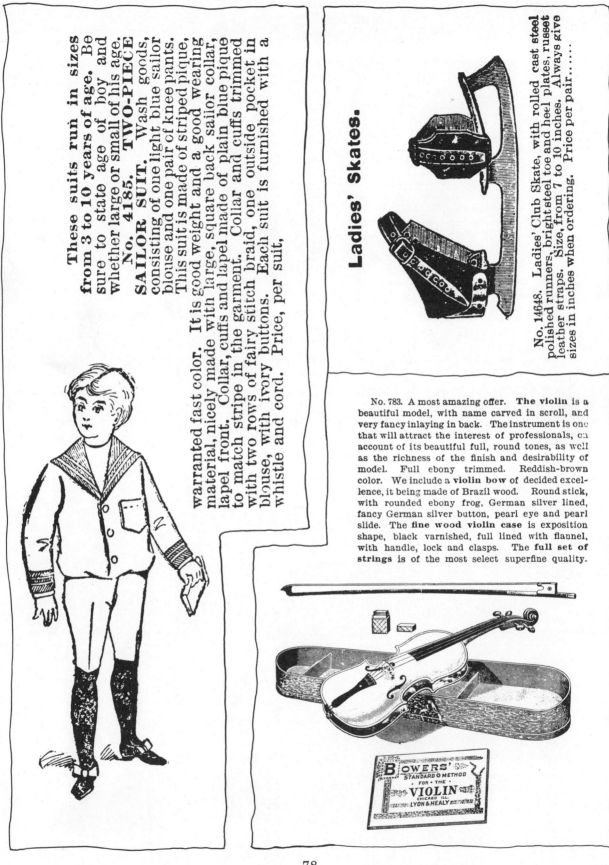

Handy Kitchen Table.

No. 9165 Among the inventions for assisting the housekeeper we know of nothing that is more convenient or satisfactory for household uses than the kitchen table we illustrate above. You can gain but very little idea from the illustration of the genuine value of this special table. It saves the tired housewife many a weary step, and keeps all the articles which can be contained therein sweet and clean. It contains, as shown in illustration, **two flour bins, one with two compartments** and the other with one, all of them large and roomy. Besides, it has **two drawers** with compartments for cutlery, etc., and **two convenient slides.** This kitchen table is made of the best hard wood with bass wood top and the size of top is 30 x 48 inches. The table is **strongly constructed** and will last a lifetime. It is well finished and presents a good appearance. It weighs about 60 lbs., and goes as second-class freight. Our special price ....

Men's Fashionable Box-Style Mackintosh Coats.

The latest and most popular style mackintosh coats made. Don't let this season go by without supplying yourself with one of these handsome and thoroughly dependable garments. Our prices will enable you to secure one of these strictly high-grade coats at a price which will clearly prove to you that we are masters of the mackintosh business in this country.

No. 21886 Men's Latest Style Double-texture, Double-breasted Box Style Mackintosh Coats. Made from fine all-wool cashmere. Seams are sewed, strapped and cemented; large velvet collar; strapped and cemented pockets; ventilated armholes; silk sewed buttonholes; first-class material and workmanship throughout. This is a strictly up-to-date garment, very new and dressy, and can be worn as an overcoat. Has a fancy plaid lining throughout Box coats will be very much in demand this season, and this is an exceptionally nice one at a very low price. We have them in plain black or navy blue. Sizes run from 36 inches to 48 inches breast measure; average length is 54 inches.

Price, each...... ....

No. 95003. **Vase Lamp.** Extra large size. Nicely proportioned and an ornament to any parlor, large climax burner. The decoration is a finely executed design of flowers in natural tints and colorings. Price.............

No. 9241 The Combination Book Case which we show in the illustration, is one of the choicest designs for the season of 1897. It is made either in oak or birch at prices given below. This book case has glass door with extra thick heavy glass and the shelves in the book case proper are removable and can be adjusted to any height desired. The very handsome hand carvings on this case add very greatly to its appearance, while the beautiful French plate mirror at the top is 10 by 14 inches in size and adds much to its attractiveness.

Razor Blade Acme Lawn Mower.

we offer a lawn mower which will compare favorably with any machine you can buy in your local market at double the price. After thorough and exacting tests we offer this lawn mower, confident that it will justify every claim we make for it. It is especially adapted to small lawns. It is extremely light, making it easy to carry from place to place. Special care has been taken in the selection of all the material entering into its construction. Simplicity of construction, easy and accurate operation, durability and finish make this undoubtedly the best light mower on the market. The mower has an improved cutter-bar of solid tool stee.. tempered and oiled. The knives have a positive shear cut and are regulated by the improved micrometer adjustment. The shafts run in phosphor bronze bearings, adding greatly to the ease and smoothness of running. New malleable iron handle brace made in one piece. Diameter of traction wheel, 7 inches; reel, 5 inches.

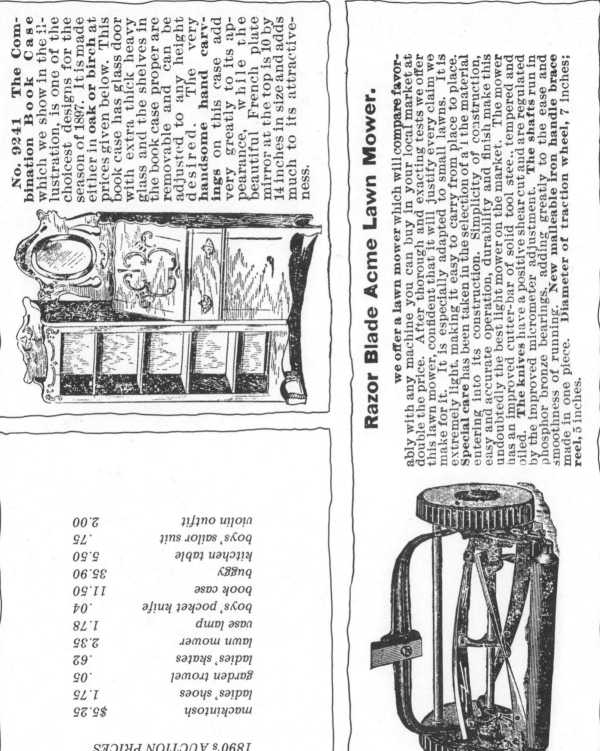

1890's AUCTION PRICES

mackintosh	$5.25
ladies' shoes	1.75
garden trowel	.05
ladies' skates	.62
lawn mower	2.35
vase lamp	1.78
boys' pocket knife	.04
book case	11.50
buggy	35.90
kitchen table	5.50
boys' sailor suit	.75
violin outfit	2.00

More telephone book history

One of the handiest backyard history tools is a commonplace book found in most homes, or hanging from a chain in one of those small glass booths down the street. It's one that we've all used many a time — the telephone book.

Even a telephone book can tell you a lot about the history of your town. About immigration to America. About the nationalities and ethnic backgrounds of the people who settled here and stayed. About how fast your town is growing. About what kinds of services your town provides.

Of course, Americans move around too much for you to be able to make really accurate guesses about what's happened in your town. But the telephone book holds some valuable clues.

Get a telephone book, right now, and look up your name. You might be in for a surprise.

So you thought you were the only "Fred Freedman" in town, huh? Instead you found out there were two of you, and seven other Freedmans (none of whom you know), to say nothing of one "Freeman" (which is just a variant of the same name). If your name is Smith, or Johnson, or Lee, or some other common name, you'd better go out and find some friends to help you count (there are about 3,200 Smiths in the Manhattan, New York telephone directory). And you might even find some long lost branches of the family.

Here are some questions you can find answers to in your city's telephone directory:

Which surname is used by the largest number of people?

How many patronyms, nicknames, occupation, place of residence, and time-of-year surnames can you find?

Can you tell which are the largest ethnic groups in your town?

And here's a tough one. Look at the addresses of a selection of people with the same nationality (Russian, Greek, Chinese, Irish, etc.) and mark where they live on a street map. Are the dots close together? Do you have any idea why that happened?

See if you can find telephone books for your community for the years 1960, 1950, 1940, and even further back. Is the population growing or getting smaller? Is there any difference in the larger ethnic groups of the community in 1940? In 1930? (And don't forget that fewer people had telephones in those days.)

Two wings, four wings, sometimes more wings

Airplanes are all beginning to look pretty much alike, but they weren't always that way. In the old days — in the 1920's, 1930's, and 1940's — airplanes (or aeroplanes, as they were called then) had very distinct personalities. Some had one motor, or two, or even three (one on the nose and one on each wing); they had two wings, sometimes four wings, and even six (three pairs stacked up on top of one another). And the motors were outside, too, where you could see them. These old planes led exciting lives. They delivered mail in all kinds of weather (the cockpits were open) and they flew people — at first only two at a time, but later more and more.

Then the war came (World War II, if you're counting) and airplanes began doing all kinds of things. They got bigger and bigger and faster and faster. They went from two engines to four, and landed in the water or even on flat-topped ships called carriers. In the 1940's jets began to appear (to the surprise of some pilots in airplanes with propellers) and they flew a lot faster and a lot higher.

You may never have seen one of these old planes, and certainly you haven't had the fun of sitting in one. With airplanes playing such an important part in our lives, it's strange that there aren't any old ones around at least to look at. Or, are there?

Airplanes don't hang very easily in museums (though there are some) and small museums are not likely to have many of them in glass cases. But there are other kinds of airplane museums, though they're not called that. They're actually little airports and private flying services, usually near small rural communities.

There you'll see planes from the past thirty years and maybe even longer ago than that. Now they're being used to spray insecticides on crops, do aerial surveys, or carry one or two people short distances. Some are even used to teach people how to fly. Others are so old they're just sitting around, sort of retired.

When you're on a long Sunday drive out to the country with your family, or on a long trip, stop for a few minutes at one of these outdoor aircraft "museums."

Take a look at the old planes.

Your parents and grandparents should be able to tell you a lot about them. (When they were growing up, those old planes were new.) I bet they'll even remember those old names like "Flying Fortress," "P-38," and "Goony Birds."

Ask the airport operator (who's probably flown all the planes there) to tell you something about them, what they are, how old each one is, and what they used to do. What are they used for now?

And find out about the pilots too. How long have they been flying? Did they used to fly mail?

Ask if you can sit in one of those biplanes with the open cockpit, and take hold of the controls . . . . There's a bit of backyard history for you!

History on a park bench

How would you like to meet and talk to a backyard historian who can remember the first motor car, or the very first airplane, the day the 1800's became the 1900's, or who listened to the crackly sounds of the very first radio broadcast through a little pair of black earphones? You would? Well there are lots of people in your neighborhood who can tell you about these first experiences and hundreds more just as exciting.

They can remember your block when it had horses and cows grazing on it. They can remember back before your dad was born, even back before your grandfather was born. They're backyard historians just like you, only *they* have been doing it for sixty, or seventy, or even eighty years. They're the older folks who you see around, who have lots of time, whose days may not be as filled with exciting things as they used to be, and who would like to share their lives with you. Eighty-year-old backyard historians are not as difficult to find as you might think. They spend sunny days in the park or perhaps finding some quiet and warmth on the bench near your school. They talk over old times with friends at senior citizens' centers; and they often work as volunteers in schools, day-care centers, hospitals, and playgrounds. They have whole lives to share, stories that will soon be lost, in fact, if they're not shared.

So the next time you see one of these very, very experienced backyard historians, stop and sit down, introduce yourself as a fellow backyard historian, and ask if they might share some of their past with you, a past that might include:

watching the first skyscraper going up

sailing on a ship powered by sails

watching your apartment building being built, or maybe helping with the building

going to a World's Fair

remembering twenty Presidents

going to a nickelodeon on Saturday afternoons

wearing stiff collars and high-top shoes

cranking the old Ford in the morning to get it started

riding a horse to school

converting their house from gas to electric lighting

riding a horse-drawn street car

fishing in the creek that used to run where the gas station is now

Whatever happened to Main Street?

Does your town have a Main Street, a Center Street, a First Avenue, or an "A" Street? If it does, I'll bet it's the oldest-looking street in town. And, if you were to look closely for dates on the cornerstones and arches along that street, you'd find that it's lined with some of the first buildings ever built in your city.

Say, come to think of it, why have those streets got names like that when they're so far off the beaten path? I hardly ever go there.

You don't, and chances are they're not the main street, center street, or first avenue any more. But they once were.

The city council may have already made plans to tear down the old part of town; it's so dingy, so colorless compared to the new, thriving downtown. No doubt there are already empty lots between the old buildings, filled with the broken bricks and rubble of a once colorful life. So before it's too late, take a walk down Main Street, and take a stroll into the past.

Here on Main Street you can close your eyes and imagine the sounds: old cars put-putting and beep-beeping their way down streets filled with the noise of horses, clanging trolley cars, and clattering carts. On the sidewalks there are women in long skirts and high-top shoes, and a bustle of workers in overalls, and clerks in stiff collars and vests. Here you can begin to understand something of your town's history if you watch carefully for the small but unmistakable bits of the past . . . .

cobblestones showing through the pavement

glimpses of old trolley tracks

an iron drinking trough for horses with a little bubbly fountain for people

elaborate cast-iron lampposts

gas lamps jutting out from old brick building fronts

little fire hydrants

This is where it all began. Perhaps, being here, you can discover by yourself how your town began.

Like people, towns have a birth, a youth, maturity, and old age. Like people, towns also have personalities; they are serious, and they laugh. Cared for, they flourish; unloved and neglected, they perish.

But unlike people, who sort of grow in every direction at once, towns tend to start at one point and grow outward.

There are any number of ways a town gets started. Lots of towns have railroad tracks running right through them. And there, just off Main Street, is the old yellow and brown station calling our attention to its role in the town's growth. It's probably very quiet now. Go take a look inside its windows and let your imagination take you back into the past . . . .

Seventy or a hundred years ago that station stood alone, nothing for miles around; alone, that is, until the cattle drives began and thousands of head of cattle arrived for shipment by train to the slaughterhouses in the big city.

Then, over the years, things changed. Bigger cattle pens were built. Hotels and saloons popped up, as did general stores, banks, firms that bought and sold cattle, and, of course, houses for all the people running these businesses.

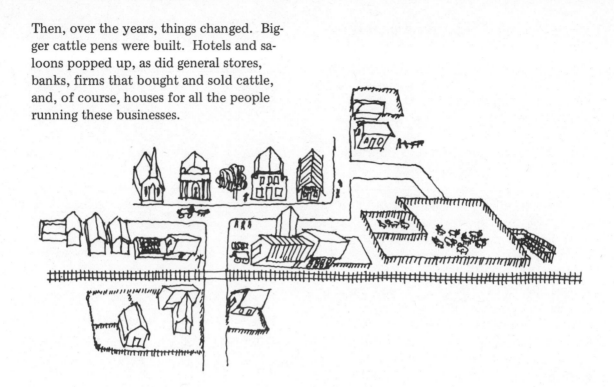

Soon manufacturers arrived to take advantage of the access to the railroad, and the town gradually became a large transportation and manufacturing center, with more houses and stores.

So, the city grows out and away from its reason for being — the railroad tracks.

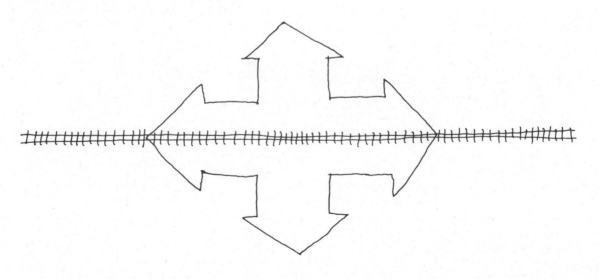

Other cities began as transportation centers too, but of a different kind — ships and shipping. These towns grew around the wharfs and docks along rivers,

or around natural harbors on the sea coast.

Even today, you can see the pattern of growth of river and seaport towns when you walk away from the port's docks and notice how the city becomes newer and newer the farther out you get.

And still another kind of city started at a
crossroads. It began with a gas station,

then a restaurant and bus stop,

then a general store,

and then — when a lot of the people who
got off the busses didn't get back on —
some houses, churches, and schools.

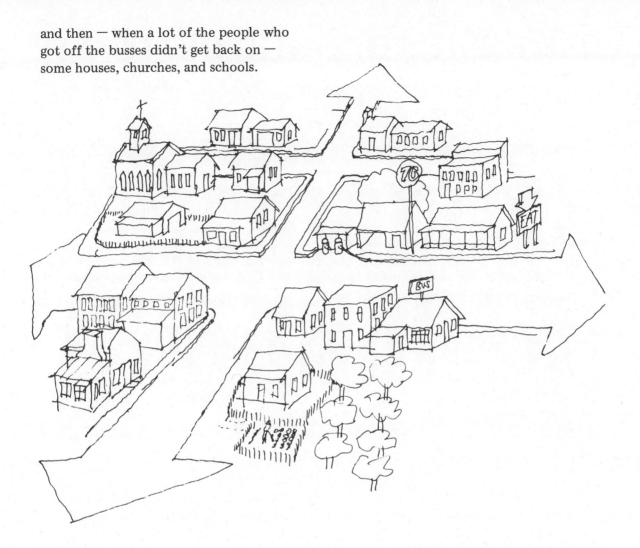

And there are still other kinds of begin-
nings for cities. There are university towns,
manufacturing cities, county seats, state
capitals, and mining towns. More recently,
whole cities have grown around recreation
areas and retirement communities.

Now, does that give you any ideas on how
your town began and why?

It may be a little difficult to tell just what
the original purpose of your city was;

things have changed so much. (For example, because railroads are not as important
as they used to be, many railroad towns
may have changed colors and become manufacturing towns.)

If you don't come up with an answer right
away, there are some suggestions coming
up for finding out more about the history
of where you live, preserving some of that
past, and most important, enjoying being
where you are.

Hanging around old town

And while you're thinking about how it all began, there's lots to look at, and do. The older parts of cities are disappearing now, being eaten up by bulldozers and the mad dash into the future. In a few years just about the only thing left in your city or town that is as much as fifty or a hundred years old may be what's in your memory. (There are groups of people around who, like you, have become interested in the history of their community and are trying to save it.)

One way to keep that memory vivid is to spend some time in the old part of town. While you're at it you can "collect" some bits and pieces of the past that interest you, and keep them alive. The first thing you can do is to make an Old Town map. It won't be a fancy map, but one you can write all over and keep notes on.

Before you leave home make sure you've got either a notepad or a clipboard with some paper in it, and a pencil, and your camera — don't forget your camera.

Where to start. If after reading that little description of how towns got started you've made a guess about yours, then start investigating that hunch. Begin at the railroad tracks (where they cross Main Street), or at the wharf, or maybe at a large meat processing plant, or stockyards. (Don't worry if your hunch turns out not to be quite right; you'll have fun anyway.)

What to do. When you get to what you think is the oldest part of town, try to make a rough map as you go along. Your first notes might look like this:

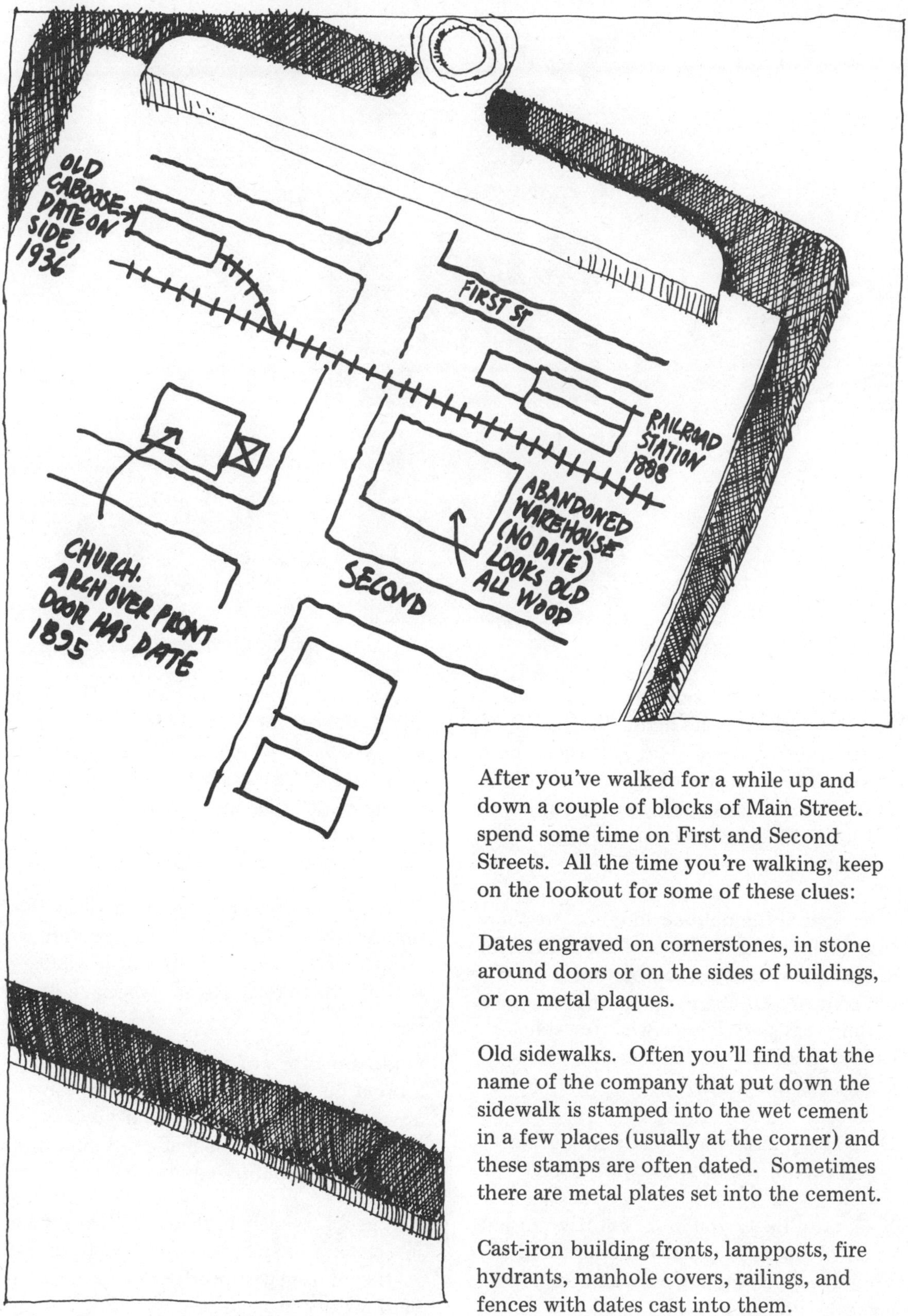

OLD CABOOSE→ DATE ON SIDE! 1936

FIRST St

RAILROAD STATION 1888

ABANDONED WAREHOUSE (NO DATE) LOOKS OLD ALL WOOD

SECOND

CHURCH. ARCH OVER FRONT DOOR HAS DATE 1895

After you've walked for a while up and down a couple of blocks of Main Street. spend some time on First and Second Streets. All the time you're walking, keep on the lookout for some of these clues:

Dates engraved on cornerstones, in stone around doors or on the sides of buildings, or on metal plaques.

Old sidewalks. Often you'll find that the name of the company that put down the sidewalk is stamped into the wet cement in a few places (usually at the corner) and these stamps are often dated. Sometimes there are metal plates set into the cement.

Cast-iron building fronts, lampposts, fire hydrants, manhole covers, railings, and fences with dates cast into them.

Old signs on the sides of buildings. What kinds of businesses are here? Industries? Warehouses? Lumber yards? Is there more of one kind of business than others? Write down some of the names you see on the old signs. Was the town once mostly of one nationality?

And clues at the railroad station. Are there maps painted on the sides of the old freight cars or at the railroad station that show the old routes? Are there any special structures around that give clues to what the trains carried in and out of town (storage tanks, grain silos, saw mills)?

Do you suppose you've really found the oldest part of the city, all by yourself?

Well, most likely you have, but if you want to check up on how you're doing there are several ways of finding out just how good a guesser you are.

Go to the city or county clerk's office (usually in the city or county office building) and ask to see the earliest map of the city they have. The clerk is there to serve the public — including amateur historians — and should be very helpful. Ask how you can get a copy of the map.

Visit your town's main library and ask the librarian where the local history section is. Ask if there are any histories of the community which might be in a special collection.

Go to a realtor's office, one which has been around for a long time. Ask if they have any old maps of the city and if you can have a copy or get one made. (Sometimes they have old photographs too.)

Tell people what you're doing. They'll get interested too and give you enough information and suggestions for dozens of backyard history projects.

A·l·l aboard!

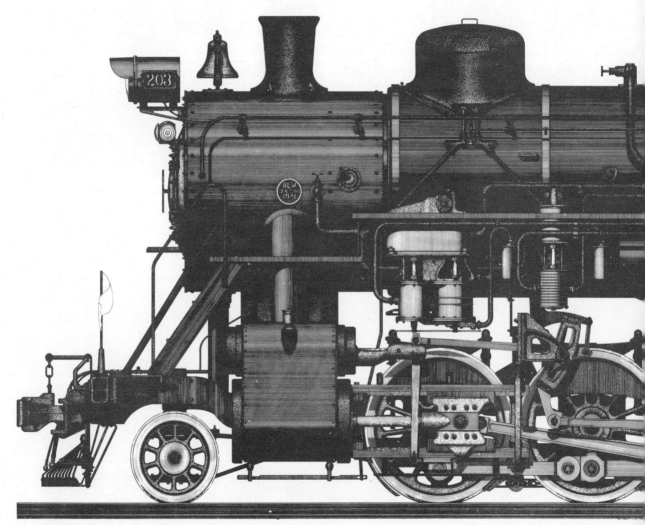

If you were to walk around an old part of Richmond, California, you'd find the usual dilapidated wooden buildings, rusty rails atop weathered gray ties, and some old railroad rolling stock with the name CASTRO POINT RAILWAY. It's a typical abandoned old railway yard . . . .

But wait a minute. What's that? There's smoke comin' out of old Number 2's stack and it's chugging toward us. The old railroad's come alive!

You're not imagining things. You can really hear the old locomotive's chuff-chuff and the clanking of the side rods, and there's no mistaking the plume of steam and puffs of coal smoke. The Castro Point Railway is one of the many old railroads around the country saved from the scrap yard by a special breed of backyard historians.

Trains probably held a special fascination for your dad and your granddad. It used to be that if you asked any boy what he wanted to be when he grew up, he'd answer either a fireman or an engineer. There were few things on earth as impressive as a steam locomotive. Somehow, it looked its job. Powerful, massive, no shiny paint or frills — it was a workhorse. And all this was controlled by two men, the engineer and the fireman. All the mechanisms, the drive rods, the valve gear, the piston rods, the brakes, were right out in the open where you could see them work. You could even see the hot coals in the firebox.

Strangely, all of this ended very quickly. Within a very few years during the early 1950's steam locomotives were replaced by streamlined, efficient diesels. Soon there were no steam locomotives anywhere to be seen. And some of us never got over it.

For the backyard historian there are some ways of revisiting the days of the steam locomotive, if not by riding one, at least by touching one, standing next to the big drivers (wheels taller than you are) and maybe sitting in the cab with your hand on the throttle.

You'll often find locomotives in parks, usually in small towns along the railroad line that was so important to the town's growth. Sometimes there'll be other things there too, a passenger car, perhaps an old caboose, and a handcar or work car.

In many large cities there are railroad parks, and museums with locomotives in them. Some of them have big collections that allow you to trace the whole history of railroads from the very beginning.

All over the country there are model railroad clubs, usually with large layouts recreating a whole railroad, the yards, shops, industries, and even cities in miniature. Here you can see a variety of locomotives and cars that you probably wouldn't be able to see any other way. Some clubs specialize in "old-timey" narrow gauge railroads, smaller equipment used for mining, logging, and short runs.

A "live steamer" is a very special kind of model, and these are sometimes found in city parks. Live steamers are model trains that actually run outside and operate on wood and coal. You've probably thought of these as "amusement park" rides, but many of the locomotives and cars have been carefully built to old plans and are actually run by members of a club.

Somewhere in your town there's a locomotive. When you find it, take some time to go visit and get acquainted with it. While you're there, climb up into the cabin and find the engineer's seat (it's the one on the right). Rest your arm on the window ledge (as the engineers used to), look down the track, and then reach up for the throttle. Move your mind back into the past as you pull back on the throttle slowly (careful, or you'll spin the drivers); before long you'll feel the heat from the firebox, smell the coal smoke, and be on your way to the "high iron."

Steam locomotives were classified by the wheel arrangements and names that were given to them. On page 100 is a guide to the kinds of steam locomotives that ran in the United States.

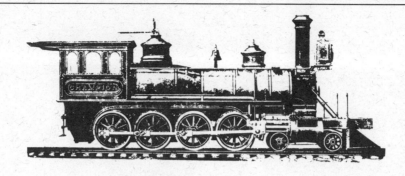

0-6-0	Six-wheel switcher
0-8-0	Eight-wheel switcher
2-6-0	Mogul
2-6-2	Prairie
2-8-0	Consolidation
2-8-2	Mikado
2-8-4	Berkshire
2-10-0	Decapod
2-10-2	Santa Fe
2-10-4	Texas
4-4-0	American
4-4-2	Atlantic
4-6-0	Ten Wheeler
4-6-2	Pacific
4-6-4	Hudson
4-8-2	Mountain
4-8-4	Niagara
4-8-8-4	Union Pacific "Big Boy"

Rubbing

Making rubbings gets the backyard historian out into the warm air and sunshine and is also an enjoyable way of preserving valuable local history.

What's a rubbing?

Well, take a coin, like a quarter or a half-dollar,

put a piece of paper on top of it,

and rub it with the side of a pencil lead.

Keep rubbing until the details get darker and darker.

There, you've just made a rubbing.

Amateur historians and museums collect rubbings of all kinds of things, like engravings, decorated tombstones, stonecutter's designs, and cornerstones. People who enjoy making rubbings often donate them to museums for their collections or for special local history exhibits. The nice thing about collecting rubbings is that you can come away with a bright record of the past to take home for your very own, yet the beautiful thing you've made the rubbing of is still there for others to see, and enjoy, and rub if they want to.

(But be careful of soft stone and old wood. These can be worn down if rubbed too much.)

Making a rubbing is really quite simple; all you need are:

some large pieces of paper (the thinner the better). You can get roll ends of newsprint from the local newspaper printing plant.

a big, fat wax crayon (with the paper removed so that you can use the edge), a big, fat lead pencil, or better yet, an inexpensive stick of artist's charcoal,

and a little whiskbroom.

Put your rubbing kit together into a knapsack or book bag and start your collection of rubbings with:

kids' names and other things people scribble into wet cement

contractors' imprints on sidewalks (sometimes this includes the date when the sidewalk was put down)

street names imprinted in sidewalks at corners

designs on iron manhole covers

cornerstones

ornamental ironwork on buildings and lampposts

bronze plaques on buildings (some tell the historical significance of the building)

bas-relief, low-relief sculpture, cast or cut into the sides of old buildings

art and lettering on monuments

tombstones

commemorative markers

cornice inscriptions and designs around doorways of old buildings. These often tell you a lot about the building's past, like when it was built, who used it (people used to put their own names on their buildings), and maybe the name of the architect, or what the building was used for originally.

If you really get into making rubbings, particularly if you're using charcoal, you'll want some kind of fixative to spray on the rubbing to keep it from smudging and wearing off when you roll it up. Art supply stores have little metal blowpipes and little bottles of fixative that you can spray all over your rubbing.

And rubbling

If you look closely at some of those old buildings you've been discovering you'll see a lot of "old-fashioned" decorations all over them, not at all like the sleek, trim architectural styles of today. Well, that was the style a hundred years ago when a lot of these old places were being built. And there's a story here that may touch on your own family history.

Beginning in the 1870's, particularly in large eastern cities like New York, an enormous number of buildings were put up to house the wave upon wave of immigrants coming into America then. Among these immigrants were skilled itinerant craftsmen, stonecutters, workers in wrought iron and sheet metal, plasterers, and woodcarvers. They went wherever there was building being done, offered their skills to the builder (who hired his workers at the job site in those days), and then moved on to the next job. Into the brick and stone they set their work . . .

ornate cornices

keystones

cornerstones

window sills and frames

friezes

pediments

carved oak doors

woodwork

tiles

mosaics

statues

stained glass

. . . fountains, stairs, columns, door arches, and grotesque, haunting gargoyles (outrageous animals which were often put on buildings as "spite cats" to annoy the people across the street, who have just ruined the view by putting up a slightly higher building).

These creations remain a record of skills that are all but lost today. These were not mass-produced pieces of pre-fab culture; though unsigned, each piece was fashioned by hands working with imagination. Often the builder would just tell the craftsman that he wanted "the head of a woman," or "pretty flowers," or just "an animal," leaving the artist considerable freedom to come up with an original idea, and often resulting in wonderfully whimsical little images.

A rubbler should always be alert to new rubble. As you walk or ride your bike on errands and to and from school, keep your eyes open for buildings about to be torn down (condemned signs, boarded-up windows, the arrival of work crews).

When you find one, check it out for interesting details. Don't just give it a casual look, but check it over carefully. The craftsmen often took private joy in putting their best work in some little, out-of-the-way nooks and crannies.

Saving these little bits of art and urban history from the wrecking ball and bulldozer is the rubbler's task. Old buildings are being reduced to rubble in many of our towns and cities. Because of this, we rubblers must work fast — but always carefully. If you think you're cut out to be a rubbler, here's how to begin . . .

PHOTO: BROOKLYN MUSEUM

Keep a record of the where and when of each piece you find, and the building it formerly decorated. Look for a date on the building. Make a rough sketch of the building's shape, if you can. You might even find the architect or builder's name somewhere on the building.

If you are unable to get the piece yourself, and the work crew is unable to get it for you, and you like the piece and want it to be saved, don't waste time.

Call the curator of local history at your city's museum, or the architecture department of a local university, or the offices of the state and local history societies. Tell them what you've found. Give them the address. And ask them to meet you there — now!

If the details are high up, get a closer look with toy binoculars or one of those cheapo telescopes.

If you find something worth keeping, write down the address and make a little sketch of exactly where it is.

If the piece can be removed *without damaging it*, size up the job, decide what tools you'll need, and borrow your family's shopping cart or a friend's wagon.

If work crews are on the job, tell them what you are doing and point out what you want. Ask them to get it for you. You'll also want to go through the rubble piles. It's important here to convince the foreman of your sincerity and the importance of your mission. This done, he'll understand your interest and the urgency of your request.

When one of these groups responds to your call (and they'll be thankful for your help), tell them that you would like to donate the piece to their collection. Suggest that they put it out with other pieces on display to alert other people to what's around them and what needs to be done.

Most city museums have special local collections and will know what to do when you call. Some even have "hot lines," numbers that you call when you have something to donate or when you know of something that needs to be rescued.

If you are unable to find a home for your "find," contact the

Brooklyn Museum
178 Eastern Parkway
Brooklyn, New York 11238

They are trying to collect architectural details from all over the United States. If they cannot use your piece, they'll send you suggestions of who might and tell you how to care for it.

Don't do rubbling for personal gain by offering your pieces for sale. Selling artifacts raises their price and value, and encourages people to rip them off for personal profit. Remember, what you have found belongs to your community's heritage and it should be preserved somewhere so it can be enjoyed and shared by all.

That's the rubbler's creed.

PHOTO: BROOKLYN MUSEUM

Rusty history

Just about now you're probably thinking that there can't possibly be any more hiding places for backyard history. You're sure you've found them all, huh? Well, how about that vacant lot down the street? You know, the one covered with weeds and rusty old junk that you go by every day without much thought. That rusty junk is history!

Back in the days when there weren't so many people living so close together, getting rid of old stuff didn't seem like much of a problem. When things broke, or wore out, or just weren't wanted any more, the simplest thing to do was just to dump them somewhere out of sight — outside the town limits, in the woods, down in an old quarry, or in a ditch alongside the road. Years

went by, generations of junk piled up, and soon each community had its own "junk museum." These were very informal museums; everyone was welcome to donate articles for the collection and, of course, the exhibits were open to the public for viewing at any time.

So, if you've never visited your local vacant-lot-rusty-junk museum, you are in for a real treat. There you'll find all sorts of wondrous things from the past. Because most of the "exhibits" have fallen apart, you can see their insides, with all those mysterious parts that make them work; and you can exercise your imagination putting them all back together again. Where else could you find things like . . .

an ancient license plate from the 1950's

a shiny chrome Packard hubcap (ca. 1935)

an oven door, complete with thermostat, from a wood-burning cook stove (ca. 1910-1920)

drive pulleys that once powered an old mill

a very early lug-wheeled farm tractor

and most of a 1930's automobile, with its classic fenders and running boards (what're those?)

and a real clue for the backyard historian: hubcaps with the trademark of the Dodge Brothers.

dash board . . .

complete with ignition switch

All going to prove that history is where you
look for it.

What's that doing there?

There are lots of old structures around cities and towns that either aren't being used anymore or are being used for something else.

Using your skills as a backyard historian, can you guess what they are?

Collecting old buildings

Well, not really collecting them — but collecting images of them and noticing the feelings old houses and buildings give us. Thinking about how they were built, what kinds of materials they're made of, their age, and why they're different, one from the other. And finding out about the people who built them and first lived in them. That kind of collecting.

If you've been doing some of the walking-around-town kind of backyard history projects, you've been looking at a lot of buildings. And that's good! Because now you're probably really seeing them for the first time, and thinking about them, too. They're no longer things you just pass on the street.

Buildings are like people in some ways, you know.

Buildings come in all sizes, like people, and they do different things. Some are muscular; others frail and slight. And they have personalities, too. Some are just plain old ordinary; some are lively and bright. New buildings look young. Old buildings get wrinkled (no kidding, look at them closely) and usually need more makeup than new ones. They have moods. And they reflect the hopes and dreams and disappointments of the people who built them.

Historians have a word for all this, it's called

Style

For the backyard historian, style is one way of telling the age of a house, for instance, and, if there are a lot of them in one place, the age of the neighborhood. And style also tells you what life was like then, what was considered "in" or "good taste." Houses were bigger when American families were bigger; houses had fewer bedrooms and got smaller in the 1930's, just after the Depression. There's a vocabulary for style, and knowing some of it makes building collecting more interesting.

Architects and historians have several ways of describing the style of a building. One simple way is to name it for the period in which it and a lot of others like it were built, like Colonial

114

or Victorian, referring to the late 1800's when Queen Victoria ruled England (and American tastes, as well)

Gilded Age

1940's Streamlined Moderne

American architects copied styles from other countries too, and these buildings are described with the names of the countries where their style originated, like

Italianate

115

Still another way to describe the style of a building is to use the names of the architects, particularly when they're famous, like Frank Lloyd Wright

or Mies van der Rohe

Louis Sullivan

American architectural styles are also named for the part of the country where they began . . .

Newport Mansion

or, maybe because they're just indescribable any other way, by the impression they give

Gingerbread

And finally, there's the "revival," the bringing back of an older style. At one time, national, state, and local government buildings were almost always a revival of the ancient Greek or Roman styles or a combination of both (which was called Greco-Roman). And there were Gothic revivals and Roman-Renaissance revivals, Spanish Colonial and many others. But you'll discover those for yourself.

So buildings not only have personalities, they have names as well.

And how do you collect old buildings? Well, the simplest way is just to become acquainted with their names so that you'll begin to know them as you travel around town.

Another way to collect them is to make little quick sketches of buildings, and maybe even include some details showing interesting stone work, or a door you like, or the design of a stained glass window.

And when you've got a camera, even a very simple one, there are lots of things you can do.

Make a sketchbook or photo album collection of old buildings in your town. A year or two from now some of them will probably be gone, and it will be fun (and sad, too) to see what they used to look like.

Make collections of sketches and photographs organized into categories like kinds of buildings, or styles, or old-new comparisons.

Things to collect:

old schools

railroad stations

country stores

old gas stations

bridges

hotels

churches

farmhouses

barns

Contact your local museum and see if they have exhibits planned on town history which might need photographs like yours.

Or, make a model of an old building.

History in a small way

Things in miniature have a certain magic about them for most people. Maybe it's seeing an immense object like a boat or a locomotive reduced to a size that fits in your hand, or maybe it's because it's so easy to grasp the wholeness of something when it's small.

If you're willing to try your hand at sketching or if you have a camera, here's a way of reducing buildings down to small size and making models of individual buildings or even a whole street of store fronts. This is a great rainy day project that can lead to the reconstruction of an entire town — if you get that caught up in it!

We'll start with a simple, four-sided structure, like an early workshop or stable from the old part of town.

First, you'll want a sketch or a photograph of each side of the building.

To do this just right, make sure that the sketch or photograph of each side is made from exactly the same distance away (you'll see why in a minute), *and* make sure, especially if you're using a camera, that *verticals* ‖ are vertical and *horizontals* ═ are horizontal in the finder.

Here's an example showing the three views you'll want to sketch or photograph.

(There are only three views because the back of this building was protected by a mean dog. Also, if you can't sketch or photograph both sides, just reverse the negative of the side you can reach and make a print for the other side.)

119

If the photograph or sketch of each of the four views has been made from exactly the same distance away, say twenty paces, each view will be in scale with the other views.

If you're sketching, you can make the pictures of the house as large as you want. If you've taken pictures of the four views, then you'll need an enlargement. Five-by-sevens are good to start with, but eight-by-tens are easier and show off better.

Now you'll need some rubber cement and some cardboard or posterboard. Coat the back of the sketches or photographs with rubber cement. And then coat the cardboard with rubber cement.

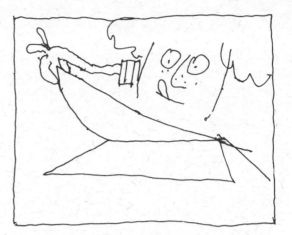

Put the pictures down on the cardboard and smooth them out (careful, you'll never get them apart again!). And then cut out each view with a single-edge razor blade or sharp knife. If the house has a sloping roof line, like this one does, cut the ends out first and then trim the sides to fit even if a little of the roof shows along the side.

Make little hinges out of scraps of cardboard or paper, and use them to glue the four sides together.

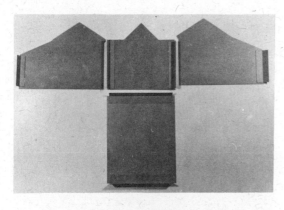

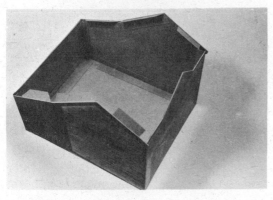

Now make a roof of gray cardboard or paper (the back of posterboard is usually just the right color).

If you really want to be clever about the roof, you can draw little shingles on it with

a felt-tip pen. Also, there will be white paper edges exposed which can be darkened with the felt-tip pen.

Using this same method, you can make models of all kinds of buildings and structures.

You could even create a whole city block!

Make a sketch or use the camera in just the same way you did before, but remember those two important details:

*be sure each picture is made from exactly the same distance away, and

*be sure verticals are vertical and horizontals are horizontal (which means this won't work for tall buildings).

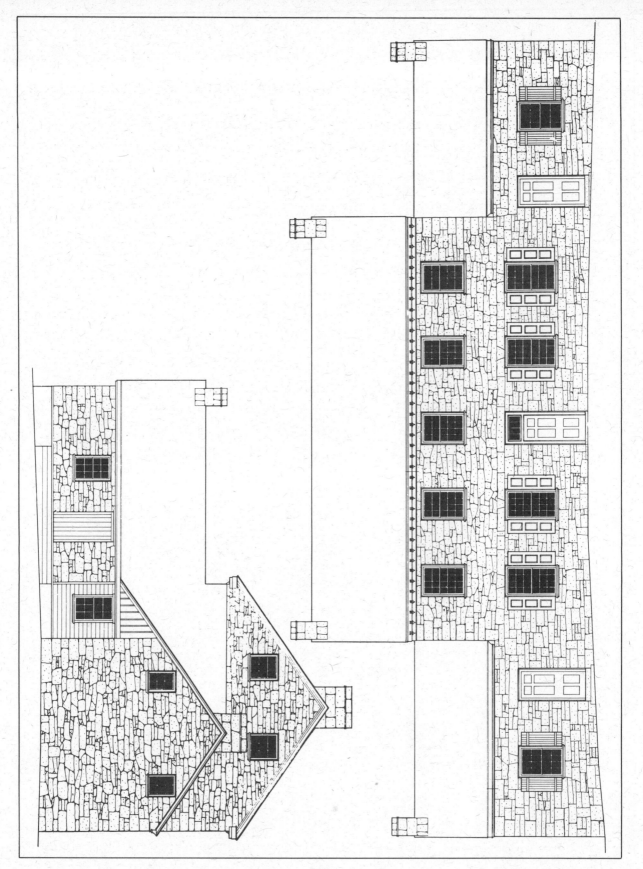

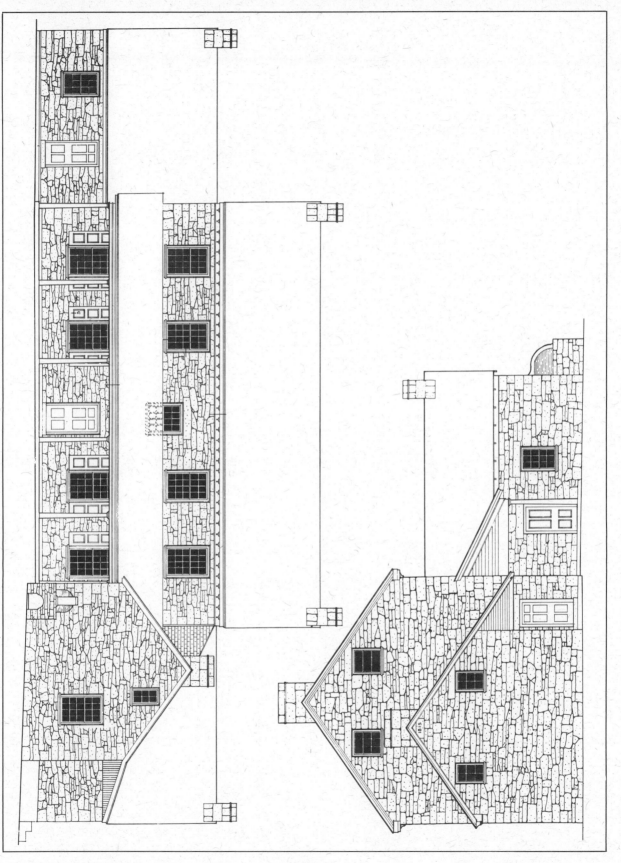

Here you are at the end of the book.

But just because you've reached the last page

doesn't mean you should stop being a backyard historian.

The nice thing about backyards is that

you can always find something interesting in them

no matter how long you go on looking.

There is no such thing as an empty backyard.

Acknowledgments

The illustration of United Airlines' 12–21 Club card on p. 21 is used by permission of United Airlines.

On p. 21, M&M ® is a registered trademark of M & M-MARS.

The New York Times front pages appearing on p. 27 are copyright © 1959 and 1962 by *The New York Times*.

The picture of Little Orphan Annie appearing on p. 27 is reprinted by permission of the New York News, Inc. All rights reserved.

The obituary appearing on p. 51 is compliments of *The Wenatchee* (Wash.) *Daily World*.

The reproduction of the jacket of BOBBSEY TWINS AT CHERRY CORNER on p. 52 is used by permission of Grosset Dunlap, Inc., publishers of THE BOBBSEY TWINS series.

The illustration of Clark Kent appearing on p. 60 is copyright © 1966 National Periodical Publications, Inc.

On pg. 62, Beechnut ® is a registered trademark of Life-Savers, Inc.

The CAMPBELL KID and accompanying jingle on p. 62 are reproduced by permission of the Campbell's Soup Company.

Smith Brothers and portraits of Smith Brothers ® on p. 62 are registered trademarks of Warner-Lambert Company.